START YOUR OWN

ETSY®

BUSINESS

Additional titles in Entrepreneur's Startup Series

Start Your Own

Entrepreneur
MAGAZINE'S

STARTUP

START YOUR OWN

ETSY®

BUSINESS

YOUR STEP-BY-STEP GUIDE TO HANDMADE SUCCESS

The Staff of Entrepreneur Media, Inc. & Jason R. Rich

Ep
Entrepreneur
PRESS®

Entrepreneur Press, Publisher
Cover Design: Andrew Welyczko
Production and Composition: Eliot House Productions

Library of Congress Cataloging-in-Publication Data
Names: Rich, Jason, author.
Title: Start your own Etsy® business: crafts, jewelry, furniture, and more / by The Staff of
    Entrepreneur Media, Inc. and Jason R. Rich.
Description: Irvine, California: Entrepreneur Media, Inc., [2017] | Series: Startup series
Identifiers: LCCN 2017007323| ISBN 978-1-59918-609-2 (alk. paper) | ISBN 1-59918-609-8
    (alk. paper)
Subjects: LCSH: Etsy® (Firm) | Selling—Handicraft. | Handicraft—Marketing. | Electronic
    commerce. | Small business—Management.
Classification: LCC HF5439.H27 R53 2017 | DDC 745.5068/8—dc23
LC record available at https://lccn.loc.gov/2017007323

Printed in the United States of America

Contents

Chapter 2

The Many Responsibilities of Online Business Operators 19

Chapter 3

Calculating Your Costs and Setting Your Prices 37

Chapter 4
Establishing Yourself as an Etsy® Seller 57

Chapter 5
Creating Your Product Listings
and Product Photography 89

Chapter 6
Promoting and Marketing Your Etsy® Shop 115

Preface

In just a few short years, Etsy® has become the largest and most successful online community for artists, crafters, artisans, and other creative people who want to showcase and sell their work. With little or no previous business experience, and absolutely no programming or website design skills, just about anyone can create a customized Etsy® shop, populate it with listings for their products, and then sell them to buyers throughout the world. Best of all, the startup costs for launching this type of business are extremely low.

Whether you're looking to earn some extra money from a hobby you already have a passion for or you have a specialized art/craft-related skill to create high-quality products others will want to buy, Etsy® offers the opportunity to transform your passion, hobby, and/or unique skill into a money-making business venture.

While some people open an Etsy® shop with the idea of making a little bit of extra money, others have discovered how to grow their Etsy®-based business into a highly profitable, full-time career. Whatever your personal goals, *Start Your Own Etsy® Business* will help you discover what it takes to become an Etsy® seller and walk you through the process of creating, managing, marketing, and advertising your own Etsy® shop. You'll also be provided with many proven strategies that will help you become successful and avoid common pitfalls.

Start Your Own Etsy® Business is not endorsed or licensed by Etsy®, Inc., so it's able to provide information from a variety of different sources, including a handful of independent, successful, and well-established Etsy® sellers, who share their exclusive insight, tips, and advice throughout this book.

As you'll discover, *Start Your Own Etsy® Business* is written for creative entrepreneurs who have an idea for products/items to sell on Etsy® but who aren't necessarily tech-savvy. It's ideal for people first getting started as an Etsy® seller, as well as for current Etsy® shop operators who want to expand or grow their business to make it more successful and profitable.

What This Book Offers

Start Your Own Etsy® Business is an easy-to-understand, nontechnical, and comprehensive "how-to" guide that will help you become an Etsy® seller and create and manage a successful Etsy® shop that showcases and sells your products. Keep in mind, this is an unofficial book that is not licensed or endorsed by Etsy®, so it's able to provide honest and reliable information based on extensive research and the actual experiences of successful Etsy® sellers.

This book will teach you how to:

▶ Properly set up your business

▶ Best utilize the Etsy® platform

▶ Set up, design, and customize your own Etsy® shop

▶ Provide tips for creating attention-getting product listings and professional-looking product photography

▶ Manage your shop from your internet-connected computer or mobile device

▶ Pinpoint your target audience

▶ Develop a viable advertising and marketing strategy for your shop

▶ Handle order fulfillment in a time- and cost-effective way

▶ Properly interact with your prospective and paying customers and always offer top-notch customer service

▶ Earn high ratings and reviews from your customers and establish yourself as a credible seller within the Etsy® community

▶ Grow your business and manage your business finances

▶ Learn about third-party services and resources that will help you operate a successful business

tip

Starting at the end of Chapter 2, "Online Business Operators Must Juggle Many Responsibilities," you'll discover an exclusive, in-depth interview with an established and successful Etsy® seller.

What truly sets this book apart, however, is that it also offers in-depth and exclusive interviews with already successful Etsy® sellers who share their advice, opinions, tips, and firsthand experiences that will help you avoid common mistakes and achieve your true potential as a seller. By reading this book, you will immediately benefit from others with extensive experience using the Etsy® platform in order to make money.

Discover What Etsy® Has to Offer

Are you an amateur or professional artisan, crafter, artist, or a person who likes to create stuff? Have you pursued your creative passion as a hobby but believe you're ready to take it to the next level, share your creations with the world, and possibly earn some extra revenue by doing this? Have you given away your creations to friends or family members as gifts, often getting told that your work is good enough to sell?

Maybe you've become so passionate about a craft that you've wound up with an extensive inventory of the items you've created but you have nothing to do with these items once they're completed.

If you've answered "yes" to any of these questions or scenarios but you don't know where to begin when it comes to selling your creations and you have no experience whatsoever operating a business, much less designing and managing an ecommerce website, then you might just have stumbled on the perfect solution—Etsy®!

In a nutshell, Etsy® is a global, online-based community and marketplace where creative entrepreneurs just like you are able to easily sell just about anything they make or curate. The Etsy® platform was established in 2005 and since then, it has grown and evolved into what it's become today.

According to Etsy®, as of mid-2017, the company provides an online home to more than 1.8 million sellers (including crafters and artisans). Unlike other services that allow sellers to showcase one listing for one item at a time, Etsy® provides all the tools necessary

► What Can Be Sold on Etsy®?

Etsy® is a global marketplace for artisans, crafters, and curators of specialty vintage items. Popular product categories featured on Etsy® include: Clothing and Accessories, Jewelry, Craft Supplies & Tools, Weddings, Entertainment, Home & Living, Kids & Baby, and Vintage. While just about anything that's handmade or crafted can be sold online through Etsy®, the service also permits certain types of vintage or antique items to be sold.

Etsy® is a continuously growing and evolving marketplace that's comprised of sellers (shop operators), as well as buyers (customers). For the seller, which could very well be you in the near future, the service provides virtually all the tools and resources needed to create and manage a successful online-based business. However, once your business is established, tools are also provided to help you successfully sell your items in the real world and accept credit and debit card payments from your customers when you showcase your creations in person, at craft fairs for example.

Etsy® is a platform that promotes what it refers to as "Creative Entrepreneurship," which means that it allows people who hand make or craft items, for example, to sell their wares within their own online-based shop that's hosted on the Etsy® online-based platform.

to create and manage an online shop, within which a seller can showcase and sell as many items as they'd like.

Thus, at any given time, the Etsy®® platform showcases in excess of 45 million items for sale and attracts an audience of more than 27.1 million active buyers who enjoy exploring the service from their computer's web browser, or using the proprietary Etsy® mobile app from their smartphone or tablet, to seek out new treasures to acquire for themselves, their home, their pet(s), their upcoming special event, or as unique gifts.

Etsy® has become the most successful platform of its kind, and in 2016, generated in excess of $2.84 billion in gross merchandise sales, because it allows its sellers to reach customers from all over the world and provides powerful tools for building and managing a shop online, yet has extremely low startup costs and requires no technical or website design skill whatsoever. As for its steady growth, in the third quarter of 2016, for example, Etsy®'s total revenue was $87.6 million, which was up 33.3 percent over the same three-month period in 2015.

What It Means to Be an Etsy® Seller

An Etsy® seller can be a crafter, painter, jewelry maker, artisan, sculptor, clothing maker, or curator of vintage items who wants to establish their own online shop on the Etsy® platform to showcase and sell their items. In other words, it's a vast online (virtual) mall that's comprised of many individually owned and operated shops. Unlike a mall in the real world, none of the shops hosted by Etsy® are chains, franchises, or operated by massive corporations. Each shop is operated by an independent "creative entrepreneur."

While Etsy® has an established and vast audience of active buyers, sellers are encouraged to do their own marketing and advertising in order to drive potential buyers from outside of the Etsy® buyer community to their shop.

Every Etsy® shop has its own unique website address (URL), as well as its own inventory of items, brand, identity, appearance, content, and shopping cart, allowing customers to make online purchases using their credit card, debit card, or a popular electronic payment service (such as PayPal or Apple Pay).

Once a seller decides what they want to sell within their shop, and then identifies their target audience, that seller has the ability to use Etsy®'s tools to customize their shop and populate it with descriptions and photos of

tip

Throughout this book, the term Etsy® shop and Etsy® store are used interchangeably. Both refer to the customized online presence a seller creates on the Etsy® online platform to showcase and sell their items.

▶ But First, A Few Basics

Etsy® offers a turnkey solution for creating and managing an online shop from which you can sell your goods and accept credit or debit card payments from your customers. You don't need to acquire a separate credit card merchant account (typically obtained from a bank or financial institution so you can accept credit card payments) or custom-program a website from scratch to get started.

As a turnkey solution, Etsy® walks you step-by-step through the shop creation process, prompting you to provide the information that's needed, such as your company name, company logo, company description, text-based product listings, and your product photos. Everything is done online via your computer's web browser, and no programming, technical know-how, or website design skills are needed.

If you know how to surf the web and use a word processor, you have much of the technical skill needed to create and manage an Etsy® shop.

Once your Etsy® shop is established, Etsy® provides many of the tools needed to promote and market your business through online advertising on Etsy®, as well as for making it so your shop and products can be found when Etsy® buyers perform searches while visiting the Etsy® service. Online advertising is highly targeted marketing that you pay for.

Etsy®'s search engine optimization (SEO) tools make it easy for Etsy®'s established buyer community to find your products and shop. That's why it's so important that your shop's text, tags, headings/titles, and other content contain appropriate keywords. These keywords get matched with the search words a prospective customer uses, and when appropriate, your business or product appears within a buyer's search results.

How to utilize these SEO tools is explained later, but it's important to understand that all advertising and marketing you do will drive traffic to your shop, and these activities are your responsibility as a seller. Beyond the advertising and SEO optimization you may opt to do directly with Etsy®, there are many opportunities to use social media services (Facebook, Twitter, Instagram, Pinterest, YouTube, etc.), as well as traditional search engine and/or website paid advertising, in order to market, advertise, and promote your Etsy® shop (your online-based business).

Through your advertising and marketing efforts, your goal is to drive as much traffic to your online shop as possible. Then, your main objective is to convert traffic (visitors to your shop)

► **But First, A Few Basics,** continued

into paying customers. It's important to understand that only a small percentage of traffic to your shop will become paying customers, so as an online business operator, one of your ongoing objectives should be to constantly improve this conversion rate.

To improve your conversion rate (the number of visitors to your shop versus the number of people who make a purchase), you'll want to target a niche audience with your marketing and advertising and then address that audience's wants, needs, and concerns directly with the content that's showcased within your shop.

When you create and launch an Etsy® shop, you become a seller (someone who runs an online-based business using the Etsy® platform to host it). The people who shop on Etsy®, and ultimately become paying customers, are referred to as buyers.

For each item you choose to sell within your Etsy® shop, it will be necessary to create a product listing for that item and then provide professional-quality product photography with each listing to showcase each item visually. Your product listings and product photography are sales tools you will use to promote and ultimately sell your products. However, the additional content you add to your Etsy® shop will also help you build a positive reputation, gain credibility, and tell your unique story.

their items. Through their Etsy® shop, a seller can also tell their unique story and develop an identifiable brand that will appeal to their target customers.

It's important to understand that when you, as a seller, launch your own Etsy®-based shop, in reality what you're doing is launching your own business, and you will need to take on all the responsibilities that being a business owner entails. Thus, the more you understand about business topics such as inventory management, customer service, bookkeeping, sales, advertising, and marketing, the bigger advantage you'll have right from the start.

Are You Prepared to Run Your Own Business?

While some Etsy® sellers have all the working business knowledge they need from day one, most take a "learn-as-they-go" approach. They keep their online-based business small at first and then slowly grow their business over time as their knowledge and skill set grow along with demand for their product(s).

Whatever business knowledge you already have will be put to good use from the start. The additional knowledge you acquire from this book and from other resources will prove invaluable. However, you'll also benefit from the firsthand experience you obtain as a business owner as you begin operating your own online business via Etsy®.

Three Key Concepts You Need to Understand Right Away

If you decide to become a seller and create your own Etsy® shop, the following are three key concepts you need to understand right from the start:

1. *No online business is a get-rich-quick scheme.* It will likely take weeks or months before you get your first sales and even longer before your business generates a profit. How long it will take to generate a steady profit is different for every Etsy® seller, based on a variety of criteria, which we'll explore shortly.
2. *When you create and launch an Etsy® shop, you're launching a legitimate business and need to run it as such,* even if you're doing this as a hobby on a part-time basis to make money. Start with a strong business foundation on which you can more easily build.
3. *To be successful, you need to develop a thorough understanding of your product(s) and why customers will want or need what you're selling.* It's equally essential that you develop a good understanding of your niche target audience.

These concepts will be explained in much more detail throughout this book, but for now, it's important that you proceed with a basic understanding to determine whether or not what you hope to sell on Etsy® offers a viable business opportunity.

Develop Realistic Expectations

First, operating an Etsy® business is not a get-rich-quick scheme. While you can establish your online business in a few hours, realistically, it could take weeks or even months before you make your first sale and even longer to begin generating a steady profit.

tip

Simply creating and launching an Etsy® shop will not guarantee a steady flow of traffic to your shop, nor will it guarantee sales. One of the skills you'll need to become proficient at is marketing and advertising your business on an ongoing basis to drive a steady flow of traffic to your shop. Many Etsy® sellers rely heavily on social media and paid online advertising to drive traffic to their shop.

The majority of Etsy® sellers start their online business on a part-time basis. Over time, however, some develop the ability to grow their business and make it a full-time career that becomes extremely profitable. It's absolutely essential that you begin this journey with realistic expectations, which this book will help you establish right from the start.

Establish Your Business Correctly from Day One

The second concept you need to understand right from the start is that as a business operator, it's important that you establish your business correctly and understand what this entails. As a business operator, you are responsible to register your business with the local, state, and/or federal government and establish it as a legal entity.

It's then your responsibility to do proper bookkeeping (on an ongoing basis), keep track of all your income and expenses, manage your inventory, communicate in a positive and professional way with your potential and existing customers, take steps to earn a profit, and pay taxes on your income. However, this is just the beginning.

As a business owner, you will be continuously juggling many different responsibilities, so it's important that you understand what these responsibilities are and set everything up correctly from day one so the foundation for your business is strong. With a strong foundation, you'll face fewer obstacles and challenges caused by common mistakes that first-time business operators often make, such as incorrectly filing state and federal tax returns or neglecting to file in a timely manner.

Being a detail-oriented and well-organized person who is good at multitasking and manageing your time will also serve you well once you become an Etsy® seller and start operating your online business.

According to Etsy®'s research published online in 2016, approximately 46 percent of all Etsy® sellers have applied for and acquired a business tax ID, and 41 percent have

warning

Launching any business, online or brick-and-mortar, requires time, effort, and at least some startup capital. While it might take only a few hours or a few days to create your Etsy® shop and populate it with product listings, this is only the first step.

Managing your shop, marketing, advertising, customer service, creating inventory, and order fulfillment are among your ongoing responsibilities that will require time and resources. Make sure you understand what running even a small online-based business entails, and only proceed if you're willing and able to make the ongoing time and financial commitment that's necessary to achieve success.

opened a business bank account. Theoretically, these percentages should both be 100 percent, which is why this book highly recommends that you establish and manage your Etsy® business as a legitimate and legal business entity to avoid tax or financial complications in the future.

Know Your Products and Your Niche Target Audience

The third essential concept you need to understand is that you, as the business operator, need to sell items that people want or need. If no demand exists, and you can't create a demand, you won't generate any sales. So, in addition to understanding your product(s) and knowing how to differentiate them in the competitive marketplace, you also must understand who your target audience is

tip

Many of the most successful Etsy® sellers pinpoint a very targeted niche audience for their product(s), which makes it much easier to find buyers who have a want or need for what you're offering. Depending on what you're selling, you may discover several unique and separate niche audiences to target.

warning

One of the biggest mistakes new Etsy® sellers make is assuming their product(s) will appeal to the mass market (absolutely everyone), and then trying to market their shop and items to everyone. This is a daunting and almost impossible task that will often cause you to waste your limited resources trying to reach people who in reality don't want or need what you're selling.

and create a plan to successfully reach this audience and drive them to your shop.

The more you know and understand about your target audience and their habits, the easier it will be to sell your products to them, reach them with your marketing message, and develop an online presence on Etsy® that caters to this audience.

Know the Importance of Ratings and Reviews

As on most popular online services (including Amazon, eBay, and iTunes, for example), buyers on Etsy® rely heavily on the ratings and reviews a seller has earned from its past customers. Once a buyer makes a purchase, they have the opportunity, using between one and five stars, to rate the seller and the product(s) they've purchased. They're also able to write a detailed review of the seller and product.

All ratings and reviews a seller receives are automatically displayed as part of their Etsy® shop. A seller with consistently good ratings and reviews earns almost instant credibility with prospective customers, while bad ratings and reviews will actually drive potential business away. Many Etsy® buyers refer to a product and seller's ratings and reviews before making their purchases. For sellers, maintaining top-notch ratings and reviews, as you'll quickly discover, is essential. Learning how to build the reputation of your Etsy®-based business is one of the skills you'll learn later in this book.

Who Is a Typical Etsy® Seller?

One of the truly great things about Etsy® is that it offers a viable business opportunity to just about everyone who has something unique, creative, and/or handcrafted to sell. The barriers to entry for this type of business are very small, and the initial time commitment and startup capital is much lower than what's required to launch most other types of business ventures.

That being said, according to Etsy®'s own research, approximately 86 percent of all Etsy® sellers are female, and they're "twice as likely to be young adults (under the age of 35) as other U.S. business owners."

For example, many successful Etsy® sellers are stay-at-home mothers or students, as well as people who pursue this as a part-time business opportunity to generate a second income that allows them to set their own hours and be their own boss.

According to research published by Etsy®, more than half of the Etsy® sellers who create and launch their own Etsy® shop have never sold their goods before, either online or in the real world. About 70 percent of sellers operate their business on a part-time basis and are able to use the revenue earned to cover at least 15 percent or more of their household expenses. For the remaining 30 percent of sellers, operating their Etsy® shop represents their full-time occupation, and some have become extremely successful pursuing this opportunity.

stat fact

A few notable statistics that Etsy® has published about its U.S. sellers indicate that the median age of a seller is 39, 86 percent are female, 56 percent have a college degree (or higher level of education), the median household income is $56,180, and 39 percent of sellers live in rural areas.

Even if you don't fit into any of these statistics, understand that Etsy® sellers come from all walks of life, all ethnic backgrounds, and all educational backgrounds, for example. What all share is a passion for whatever craft or artisanal skill they possess.

What's great about operating an Etsy® shop is that it can be run from home, and most choose to sell items they create using a skill set that's self-taught. Because the cost of entry is so low, most Etsy® sellers are able to successfully launch their business using their own savings. Etsy® reports that less than 1 percent of first-time sellers need to acquire some type of loan from a bank or financial institution to get started.

Furthermore, once an Etsy®-based business is established, the majority of sellers are able to manage their business on their own and from their home. Those who do require additional help often seek advice and assistance from unpaid friends and family members. Only about 5 percent of Etsy® sellers take advantage of paid help on an ongoing basis. Others hire freelancers with specialized skills and experience only when some specific type of assistance is needed.

Running a Business Requires Your Time

One concept that can't be stressed enough as you get started with your business is that becoming an Etsy® seller and shop operator will take time and resources. If you already have a full-time job and family responsibilities, you'll need to find time each and every day to handle the responsibilities associated with your Etsy® business.

Again, depending on your business and how popular it becomes, the time commitment might be just a few minutes, or one or two hours per day, or a few days per week. However, you could wind up needing to dedicate three to five hours per day (or more), to handle all your new business-related responsibilities.

Out of all the time you dedicate to running your Etsy® business, be aware that on average, Etsy® sellers spend about half this time making whatever it is they'll be selling.

You'll also need to spend additional time handling tasks such as inventory management, marketing/advertising, communicating with potential and existing customers, handling bookkeeping and accounting tasks, fulfilling and shipping your orders, and actually managing the Etsy® shop.

Some of the Etsy® shop management-related responsibilities will include writing and updating your product listings, managing the overall appearance and other content within the shop, taking or acquiring professional-quality product photography, and handling search engine optimization tasks that will help buyers find your shop.

How much time you need to dedicate to each of these tasks will depend a lot on your personal skill set and existing experience, as well as the type of business you'll be operating, what you're selling, and how successful and popular your business becomes. You'll learn from this book how to successfully handle the majority of these tasks, plus discover additional resources that will help you acquire or develop the skills you will ultimately need.

▶ Find the Help You Need Early On

While only a small percentage of Etsy® shop operators hire paid help on an ongoing basis, if you don't possess all the skills and knowledge you'll need to get the business up and running correctly, you may need to hire freelance help initially so that everything is done correctly.

Depending on your business, you might want to or need to hire a freelance graphic designer/ artist to create your company logo, a photographer to take your professional-quality product shots, an accountant to help you establish your business entity and set up your bookkeeping system (and then file your tax returns each year), and/or someone with online marketing experience to help you develop and implement a successful paid advertising and marketing campaign right from the start.

Depending on your business, you may also require the services of a lawyer to help you file trademarks, copyrights, or patents to protect your work and intellectual properties, although by using tools and services found online, you may be able to learn how to handle these tasks on your own.

For example, as a lower cost alternative to hiring a lawyer, you could use an online, fee-based service such as LegalZoom.com (www.legalzoom.com), to help you incorporate or establish your own legal business entity, plus file your own copyright, trademark, and/or patent applications, as needed.

Help you need can come from an unpaid friend or family member, or you may want to or need to hire someone on a freelance basis to assist you with specific tasks. These freelancers can be paid by the hour, or on a project-by-project basis, and can be found through word-of-mouth or from online services such as Upwork (www.upwork.com).

Depending on your needs, like many successful Etsy® sellers, you may also tap the talents of paid or unpaid college interns as a low-cost way to obtain specialized assistance or guidance in areas where you lack some of the necessary specialized knowledge, skill, or experience.

Early on, as you define your business and create your business plan, think about what skills, knowledge, and experience you already possess and what areas of running a business you don't yet have that's needed to achieve success. Then, determine how you can find and tap into the resources you need when you need them.

Instead of waiting until you run into a problem or make costly mistakes before you seek the help you need, consider determining your needs and acquiring the necessary assistance right from the start. This approach can ultimately save you time, money, and a lot of aggravation.

Every Successful Etsy® Business Starts with a Great Idea and Planning

Regardless of what you opt to sell on Etsy®, chances are you'll encounter a lot of competition—not just from other Etsy® sellers, but from other online and real-world business operators. Learning how to deal with your competition, set yourself and your product(s) apart, and provide a superior shopping experience for your customers are what will ultimately allow you to achieve success.

It all starts, however, with a passion for what you want to do as well as a good idea. Think carefully about what you want to sell through Etsy®. Is it something that you'll be making yourself? What do your product(s) offer that's innovative, unique, or that somehow sets it apart from similar products already on the market?

If you'll be selling your handcrafted jewelry, for example, what makes your jewelry line different from all the other handcrafted jewelry that's already being sold on Etsy® or the jewelry that customers can readily purchase from retail jewelry shops and department stores, for example?

It's important for you to analyze your product(s) carefully and consider what makes them special. Next, think about the amount of time it takes for you to create each product and exactly what your cost of goods will be. Next, calculate how much money you want to earn for your time, plus consider all the operating expenses you'll have for your business.

Dollars and Sense

Now, it's time to crunch some numbers. Based on the value of your time (whether it's $5, $10, or $50 per hour, for example), and your cost of goods to create the item(s) you'll be selling, how much will you need to charge per item to just break even?

How much will you need to charge to earn a profit after covering all your business expenses, including your Etsy® listing fees, product photography costs, product packaging costs, advertising/marketing expenses, and the acquisition of equipment you'll need, for example?

Consider what your competition is currently charging for similar products. Can you price your items in a competitive way? If you're forced to charge more for your items than your competition, can you justify the added cost, and will you be able to convince your customers to pay a premium price for what you'll be offering?

Based on what you perceive to be the demand from the niche target audience(s) you identify for your product(s), will you be able to generate enough sales each month to cover your costs and time, plus generate a profit?

As you begin to address these questions, consider developing a formal business plan.

The All-Important Business Plan

Your business plan should clearly define your company objectives, describe your products, outline all your costs and expenses, and describe how you'll operate your business.

▶ What to Include in Your Business Plan

A business plan is a written document that forces you to create a long-term plan for your venture and consider a wide range of factors that will contribute to its success or demise. A business plan will help you understand your strengths and weaknesses as a business operator and predict what challenges, expenses, and responsibilities you will likely encounter as your business grows.

Creating a business plan forces you to:

- ▶ Analyze the viability of your product idea(s)
- ▶ Identify your target audience(s)
- ▶ Examine your competition
- ▶ Predict demand for your products
- ▶ Calculate your anticipated business-related expenses
- ▶ Determine what equipment and supplies you'll need
- ▶ Analyze what skills, knowledge, and experience you already have, and identify what additional skills or knowledge you'll need to acquire (or the type of professionals you'll need to hire on a freelance basis) to help you properly establish and run your business, starting from day one
- ▶ Create a preliminary marketing and advertising plan
- ▶ Make financial projections
- ▶ Create a master to-do list that needs to be completed as you set up the business

The more time and effort you put into the creation of your business plan upfront, the better prepared you'll be when it comes to handling a wide range of business tasks and overcoming any challenges or unexpected obstacles you may encounter. A business plan can also help you develop realistic expectations for your business.

Because you probably won't be seeking a formal business loan or investors, your business plan does not have to be as thorough or detailed as a typical business plan might otherwise need to be. However, it should be created in a way that provides you with a roadmap to follow so you understand your short- and long-term objectives.

To help you draft a business plan, you can acquire specialized software. There are also countless online guides and templates that you can use to speed up the business plan creation process. For example, starting at $19.95 per month, LivePlan (www.liveplan.com) offers more than 500 business plan templates and guides you step-by-step through the business plan writing process.

Free resources for creating a business plan are also provided online by the U.S. Small Business Administration (www.sba.gov/starting-business/write-your-business-plan). Here, not only will you find a text-based tutorial for creating a business plan, you can also watch an instructional video and take advantage of free, interactive tools.

Figure out Which Product(s) You'll Be Selling

Based on what you plan to sell, does your product fit nicely onto the Etsy® platform? Will you be able to use the tools and resources offered by Etsy® to create and establish an Etsy® shop that will allow you to properly showcase and sell your items?

The best way to determine this is to go online, visit Etsy®, and invest time exploring the service. Visit a handful of Etsy® shops, make a few purchases, interact with a few sellers, and research who your competition on Etsy® might be.

As you explore the Etsy® platform, consider how you'll populate and customize your shop. Think about how you'll use the tools available to you to develop and promote your company's unique brand, and think about how your product descriptions, product photos, company logo, and other content will be displayed. Will the shop you want to establish properly cater to your target audience?

Regardless of what you'll be selling on Etsy®, you will not have to reinvent the wheel, so to speak, when creating your shop. Take advantage of the tools and resources Etsy® offers to help you create and manage your shop using tools and techniques that have been proven to be successful.

tip

After reading this book, read the online-based *Etsy® Seller Handbook* (www.Etsy.com/seller-handbook), which explains how to utilize all the tools and resources Etsy® offers to help you achieve success as a seller. From Etsy®'s website, you'll also discover blog posts, articles, user forums, free video webinars, and an interactive Help Center, all of which are designed to help Etsy® sellers achieve success.

Start with a Passion

If you ask any super successful business leader how they achieved their success, chances are they'll respond by saying, "I've always had a true passion for my work." The same is definitely true among Etsy® sellers, as you'll discover by reading the interviews that are featured at the end of each of this book's chapters (starting with Chapter 2).

To achieve long-term success operating an Etsy® shop, start with a passion for being a crafter, artist, artisan, or curator for whatever it is you'll be selling. It's important that you truly love making whatever it is you'll be selling because when your business becomes successful, a lot of your time will ultimately be spent creating or making your inventory on an ongoing basis.

Next, make sure you have a passion for becoming an entrepreneur. This means that you have the drive, dedication, and willingness to invest your time, resources, and effort toward building and managing your own successful business.

As an entrepreneur operating a shop on Etsy®, you work for yourself—not for Etsy®. There's nobody to tell you what to do, force you to meet deadlines, or make sure you handle all your business responsibilities correctly. While not every task you're responsible to handle will be fun, it's important that you don't hedge your responsibilities or take shortcuts.

The good news is while you're operating your own online Etsy® business, you're never alone. There's an entire team at Etsy® that's willing and able to assist you, plus there's a vast and ever-growing community of Etsy® sellers that you can learn from and communicate with.

In fact, it's the tools and resources that Etsy® offers to sellers, as well as the established community of sellers and buyers that exist on the platform, that set Etsy® apart from its competition and make it an ideal place for many artisans, crafters, and artists, for example, to establish their business in the form of an Etsy® shop.

Without a passion for whatever it is you'll be selling, as well as a passion for operating your own business, you'll find it very difficult to motivate yourself day after day to handle your responsibilities as a business owner and maintain a positive attitude, especially when interacting with your prospective and existing customers.

So, before you proceed any further, ask yourself two simple questions. First, "Do I truly love creating whatever it is I will be selling?" And second, "Will I love sharing my talent and work with prospective customers, sharing my story, and enticing these people to buy my products?"

If you answered "yes" to these two questions, then you're already a really good candidate to become one of the next successful sellers on Etsy®! However, if you answered "no" to either or both of these questions, do some serious soul searching and reevaluate your goals prior to committing yourself to establishing your own business.

There are Other Places for Sellers to Sell

Without a doubt, Etsy® has become the world's largest and most successful online community and platform for "creative entrepreneurs" to sell their goods through their own online shop. Etsy® is not, however, your only option for selling your goods online.

As an independent business operator, crafter, artisan, or artist, you always have the option to create and manage your own stand-alone ecommerce website (which is a website that allows you to sell items online, as opposed to just convey information to website visitors).

fun fact

To compete directly with Etsy®, Amazon has established a service called Amazon Handmade (www.amazon.com/handmade), which is separate from the main Amazon.com shopping service. Using the familiar Amazon interface, Amazon Handmade also allows artisans, crafters, and artists to establish their own online shop to sell their creations.

If you choose to create and manage your own online business via your own website, there are many online turnkey solutions that offer the tools you need to create and manage a website. To find these services, enter the search phrase "ecommerce turnkey solution" using any search engine, such as Yahoo! or Google.

You'll discover services from companies such as Google, Yahoo!, Amazon, eBay, GoDaddy, Intuit, Shopify, Big Commerce, Wix, Volusion, and countless others that offer tools and resources for building an ecommerce website without needing to possess any graphic design or website programming skills.

Established online services such as Amazon and eBay also allow independent sellers to showcase and sell items online, but these services don't cater to specifically crafters, artists, or artisans.

Some Etsy® sellers have previously either sold their goods in person at local craft shows or have already established limited distribution by selling their items through local consignment shops or retail shops. If this is the case for you, there's no need to stop these endeavors if they've been successful for you.

In fact, you'll probably discover that having a presence on Etsy® allows you to attract customers whom you have met at craft shows, for example, but who didn't make a purchase during the show itself. By promoting your Etsy® shop at craft shows and other such events, you're able to drive future traffic to your online shop.

Etsy® now offers tools for making in-person credit or debit card sales in a way that integrates seamlessly with your Etsy® shop when it comes to inventory management and finances, for example. To learn more about these tools and resources, visit www.Etsy.com/reader.

Without having to learn any website programming or graphic design skills, what you'll discover is that Etsy®'s easy-to-use services and tools cater to all sellers, regardless of how established and experienced they already are as businesspeople.

tip

Other Etsy® competitors you might want to look into before choosing Etsy® to host your shop include: DaWanda (www. dawanda.com), Bonanza (www.bonanza.com/ sell_products_online), Zibbet (www.zibbet.com/ sell), or iCraft Gifts (www. icraftgifts.com/sell.php).

Each service offers its own collection of tools and resources for sellers and charges its own set of fees. Choose a service that's competitively priced, offers the tools and resources you will find the most useful, and that will allow you to showcase your products in the best possible way.

The Many Responsibilities of Online Business Operators

Being a business operator comes with a broad range of responsibilities, the majority of which are common to all businesses, but some will be specific to what you plan to sell on Etsy®.

Once you decide to create an Etsy® shop, one of your first steps should be to establish yourself as a legal business

tip

Much of what's included in this chapter will help you establish a strong foundation for your business, which, along with an established plan, will help you move forward in a more organized way, avoid common pitfalls and mistakes, and ultimately save you time, money, and aggravation in the future.

entity. Etsy® allows you to set up a shop and begin selling items by classifying your activity as a "hobby." However, once you begin earning money, if you're based in the United States, the U.S. government expects you to pay taxes on that income.

Establishing Yourself as a Legal Business Entity

If you're based within the United States, refer to the Internal Revenue Service's website (www.irs.gov/uac/business-or-hobby-answer-has-implications-for-deductions) to determine when and if you need to establish yourself as a legal business entity or classify your income from selling items on Etsy® as a hobby. You can (and should) also consult with a business lawyer or accountant.

The following information from the IRS's website provides the necessary guidelines:

In order to make this determination, taxpayers should consider the following factors:

▶ Does the time and effort put into the activity indicate an intention to make a profit?

▶ Does the taxpayer depend on income from the activity?

▶ If there are losses, are they due to circumstances beyond the taxpayer's control, or did they occur in the startup phase of the business?

▶ Has the taxpayer changed methods of operation to improve profitability?

▶ Does the taxpayer or his/her advisors have the knowledge needed to carry on the activity as a successful business?

▶ Has the taxpayer made a profit in similar activities in the past?

▶ Does the activity make a profit in some years?

warning

Keep in mind, once your business begins earning a profit (or generates significant losses) if you misrepresent your earnings or losses on your tax returns, you could be subject to costly penalties and interest.

▶ Can the taxpayer expect to make a profit in the future from the appreciation of assets used in the activity?

The IRS presumes that an activity is carried on for profit if it makes a profit during at least three of the last five tax years, including the current year.

The easiest type of business entity to set up within the United States is called a DBA (Doing Business As). As long as you are the sole proprietor of the business, you can register your business as a DBA using your company's name by filling out a few forms and paying a small fee to your state. The basic requirements for establishing a DBA, the cost, and what forms must be completed vary by state. However, the process is very inexpensive and quick.

Once you establish your business, it will ultimately be necessary to obtain a Tax Identification Number (TIN) from the IRS. Depending on the type of business entity you establish, the process for doing this varies, but part of the process involves completing the SS-4 Form from the IRS (www.irs.gov/pub/irs-pdf/fss4.pdf). If you will be operating your business as a DBA, you will be reporting business income on your individual tax return and can typically use your Social Security number as your Tax ID number.

After you have established your business as a legal entity and have acquired a TIN, you are able to open a business bank account with any bank or financial institution. You will also find it easier when you set up accounts with your suppliers and will be able to purchase supplies at wholesale prices for creating whatever it is you'll be selling on Etsy®.

tip

As a business owner in the United States, there are multiple options for establishing your business as a legal entity. The most appropriate option to choose will depend on the type of business you will be operating. Each has its own tax requirements and legal ramifications.

For the majority of Etsy® sellers, a DBA is the fastest and easiest option, at least to get started. However, you should consult with a business lawyer or accountant to see if establishing your business as an LLC (limited liability corporation), S-Corporation, C-Corporation, nonprofit, or LP (limited partnership), for example, might serve you better in the long run.

Figure Out What Skills You Still Need to Acquire

As an Etsy® seller, chances are you will be making items and then selling them online through your Etsy® shop and perhaps in person at craft fairs. You might even establish retail distribution for your items through retail boutiques or consignment shops, for example.

In addition to mastering the skills needed to create whatever it is you'll be selling, running an Etsy® business will require you to become proficient in other areas as well. If you don't have the necessary skills, at least initially, consider working with people who do so you can get your business up and running in the most efficient way possible without making costly and time-consuming mistakes.

The following sections discuss some of the basic skills and knowledge that you'll want to have as you begin running your Etsy® business. They are presented in alphabetical order—not in their order of importance.

Basic Accounting and Bookkeeping

It's important that you keep track of your expenses, income, and all other finances pertaining to your business. Ideally, you should begin utilizing accounting and bookkeeping software, such as QuickBooks (https://quickbooks.intuit.com/smallbusiness) on your PC or Mac to do this on an ongoing basis. Once all your financial information is recorded in QuickBooks, you can easily supply this data to an accountant when it comes to preparing your tax returns.

tip

There are many online-based services that, for a small fee (in addition to your state's filing fees), allow you to complete and file your DBA forms with the appropriate government agency. For example, there's SimpleFilings (www.simplefilings.com/state-dba/home.php), GovSimplified (www.taxid-gov.us), and Legalzoom (www.legalzoom.com/business/business-formation/dba-overview.html).

Customer Service

Regardless of what you're selling, you will need to interact with your potential and paying customers. This communication will often be via email but could be on the phone as well. If you're selling items at a crafts fair, in-person interaction is required. Understanding how to interact with your customers in a professional, polite, and nonconfrontational way is essential, especially if something goes wrong and a customer becomes dissatisfied with their shopping experience or your product(s).

Inventory Management

When you're selling items to customers, it's important that you maintain proper inventory so you never wind up in a back-order situation and force paying customers to wait an extended

▶ Good Customer Service Means Making Exceptions to Your Rules

When establishing your Etsy® shop, you'll want to clearly spell out any warranties or guarantees that you offer, your shipping policy, order fulfillment timeline, as well as your return or exchange policy. All this information should be prominently displayed. However, there will be times when you need to bend the rules due to a customer's extenuating circumstances.

Offering superior and personalized customer service is not just important, but absolutely essential when someone needs to return or exchange an item. For example, if you have a 15-day return policy but someone contacts you 18 days after receiving their item, explains that they were traveling on a business trip and still needs to return the item for a refund or exchange, as the business operator, you'll want to bend the rules and allow for the late return or exchange.

You might respond to the request by saying, "Our company policy is that we only accept returns or changes within 15 days; however, this one time, I am willing to make an exception due to your extenuating circumstances. Please return the product for a refund, or let me know which item you'd like to exchange it for."

Providing top-notch customer service also requires you to respond to customer questions within hours, not days or weeks; fulfill incoming orders quickly; and include a personalized thank-you note, for example, within the packaging when you ship each order.

As a small-business operator, one of your goals should be to humanize your business. Always provide your prospective and paying customers with personalized and prompt attention.

period to receive their purchases. This will result in lost sales and unhappy customers. Once a customer places an order, they expect it to ship almost immediately unless it is a custom item. Failure to meet shipping expectations will result in you receiving a poor rating and review or the loss of a customer who will simply cancel their order and shop elsewhere.

Advertising Skills

Most Etsy® sellers agree that in addition to the traffic that's organically driven to your shop as a result of buyers entering keywords or search phrases that are related to your business or products into the Etsy® search field, as a business operator, you need to market and promote your shop to your target (niche) audiences on an ongoing basis. Doing this will allow you

▶ Many Inventory Management Tools Are Available

Whether you sell one item or several hundred items, your inventory management system should allow you to accurately keep track of information such as what's in stock, what's on order, what needs to be made, and what your projected inventory needs will be in the weeks and months ahead.

In addition to the inventory management tools offered online by Etsy®, there are third-party software applications you can use to handle inventory management. For example, the QuickBooks business accounting software offers inventory management tools, including QuickBooks Point of Sale (www.intuitpayments.com/seg/brand/all/qb-pointofsale).

Depending on the size of your business and the number of products you sell, additional software tools available to you include: EcomDash Inventory Tracking Software (www.ecomdash.com/inventory-management), Fishbowl Small Business Inventory (www.fishbowlinventory.com/articles/inventory-management/small-business-inventory-software), and JumpStock™ Inventory Management (www.jumptech.com/products/jumpstock).

To find additional inventory management software applications and mobile apps, enter the search phrase "Inventory Management Software for Etsy®" or "Inventory Management Software for Small Business," using any search engine, such as Yahoo! or Google.

Another less costly option is to acquire a Microsoft Excel template that's designed for inventory management. In fact, you'll even find some available online that are designed specifically for Etsy® sellers. Two of these include Indzara (www.Etsy.com/listing/235377094/retail-inventory-and-sales-manager-excel) and ReferenceSystems (www.Etsy.com/listing/208599426/stock-inventory-tracking-customer-vendor).

to continuously drive traffic to your shop. Chapter 6, "Promoting and Marketing Your Etsy® Shop," explains some of the popular and most effective paid advertising options.

Photography Skills

When you operate an online business and sell products online, your customers cannot touch, smell, or interact with your items. Instead, they must rely on your written product descriptions and your product photos when making their purchasing decision. That being said, displaying crystal-clear, professional-quality, and extremely detailed product photos within your Etsy® shop is absolutely essential. There is a direct correlation between having high-quality, detailed images and making sales. You'll learn more about product photography from Chapter 5, "Creating Your Product Listings and Product Photography," but for now, understand that if you don't have the photography skill and equipment needed to take your own product shots, you will need to solicit the help of a semi-professional or professional photographer.

Social Media Skills

Paid online advertising is a proven way to drive highly targeted traffic to your Etsy® shop. However, this costs money. In addition to, or instead of, relying on paid ads, consider establishing a presence for your business on popular social media services, including Facebook, Twitter, Instagram, Pinterest, and/or YouTube. Using social media is free, but it does require a significant time commitment to build an online audience and populate your social media accounts with fresh and informative content on an ongoing basis. Refer to Chapter 6 for more information about how to use social media as a powerful marketing tool.

Writing Skills

Writing is an important skill when operating any online business. As you establish and then manage your Etsy® shop, you will need to write clear, concise, detailed, informative, and attention-getting product descriptions, as well as compose and share information about you and your company. Explain your company's various policies and tell a compelling story about your brand. Thus, it's essential that anything you publish be clearly written, customized for your target audience, and free of spelling and grammatical errors. Writing skills are also needed to compose product manuals (if applicable), promotional newsletters or blog posts, and for generating personalized correspondence with your potential and paying customers.

tip

Paid advertising can be done in the real world, using newspaper or magazine ads, for example. However, a more cost-effective way to target your audience is through the use of paid online advertising. Learning how to create and manage online ad campaigns that generate results is a skill unto itself and one that you'll definitely want to acquire early on.

Some of your online advertising options include: Etsy® advertising (www.Etsy.com/help/article/49716927767); Facebook advertising (www.facebook.com/business); and Google AdWords advertising (www.google.com/AdWords), all of which are explained in Chapter 6.

► Professional-Quality Product Photos Are Essential

One of the biggest mistakes first-time Etsy® sellers often make is establishing their shop and populating it with great products, but showcasing those products using poor-quality, badly lit, blurry, or unprofessional-looking product photography. Doing this is a guaranteed way to demonstrate a lack of professionalism and dedication to your business, tarnish your credibility, and drive potential customers away from making a purchase.

Invest the time and money that's needed to acquire the best product photography possible, and then showcase each of your products from multiple angles or perspectives, using up to five detailed product photos.

As you'll learn from Chapter 5, there are two main types of product photos. An image can showcase just your product with a simple background (typically white), or it can be a lifestyle photo that shows your product being used or worn in the real world, for example. As an Etsy® seller, you'll probably want to use both types of product shots to properly showcase your items.

Running a Business Takes Time

As mentioned in Chapter 1, make sure you have enough time in your schedule to take on the responsibilities of operating an Etsy® business, even on a part-time basis. This is especially true if you already have a full-time job and family responsibilities.

It will take time to initially establish your Etsy® shop and get it up and running, and then on an ongoing basis you will need to invest time each day to manage the business. It takes time to respond to customer and potential customer inquiries, fulfill and ship orders, manage your shop, promote your business, and handle all the related tasks. All this is in addition to the time required to create your handcrafted inventory.

Plus, until your business becomes established and begins receiving orders, you may need to put in weeks or months of hard work before earning any money. How much time you will need to invest in your business will

tip

If you don't have the necessary writing skills, consider hiring a freelance writer to create your text-based content for you. At the very least, find someone who is capable of proofreading your work before you publish it online. You can hire a professional editor or proofreader from a service such as Upwork (www.upwork.com).

► How to Acquire the Skills You Need

If you don't yet possess some of the skills needed to successfully operate your Etsy® business, you have a few options. You can learn as you go but run the risk of making potentially costly and time-consuming mistakes, or you can begin learning the necessary skills by participating in online or real-world classes, watching instructional videos, reading how-to books, and taking advantage of the free resources on Etsy® including the *Etsy® Seller Handbook* (www.Etsy.com/seller-handbook).

Plenty of free instructional videos are available from YouTube (www.YouTube.com), while free online classes covering a wide range of business topics are available from Apple's iTunes U service (www.apple.com/education/itunes-u). Open Culture (www.openculture.com/business_free_courses) offers more than 150 free online classes on small-business subjects.

There are also countless universities that offer online business classes that you can take at your own pace, as well as low-cost, in-person adult education classes that are taught in many cities across America.

Another option is to hire freelancers with specialized skills who can help you get your business established. You will need to pay freelancers by the hour, or on a project-by-project basis, to assist you with specific and specialized tasks. However, if you have friends or family members with specific skills, consider asking for their assistance on a volunteer basis, or contact a local college or university to see if you can utilize unpaid interns to help you accomplish certain tasks.

You should not have to spend a fortune to acquire the knowledge or assistance you need, especially when you're first establishing your business.

vary greatly, based on a wide range of factors. However, before you get started, make sure you develop realistic expectations and understand the time investment that's required.

Make sure the responsibilities of operating your Etsy® shop will not infringe on your ability to meet your full-time job responsibilities, and that your family understands that you will need to make some sacrifices that may involve spending less time with them to run your business.

Most Etsy® sellers are able to adapt to the time demands required to operate their shop without making too many sacrifices in other areas of their life. However, it could take you some time to develop the time management skills and discipline needed to successfully juggle all your new responsibilities efficiently.

tip

The more organized you are in predicting and planning what you need to accomplish each day or week, the easier time you'll have juggling your personal, work, and Etsy® shop responsibilities.

One way you can maximize your time is to use scheduling software on your computer or mobile device. Preplan, as much as possible, how you'll allocate your time each day. Develop a schedule for meeting each of your responsibilities. If you're not tech-savvy, consider using a printed planner/calendar from a company such as Day-Timer (www.daytimer.com), Levenger (www.levenger.com), or FranklinCovey (https://franklinplanner.fcorgp.com/store).

Some Etsy® sellers respond to their incoming customer inquiries at designated times throughout the day. They then have a time allocated each day to fill and ship new orders, as well as time set aside each week to create their inventory, update their shop content, and handle other specific tasks.

Acquiring the Equipment and Supplies You Will Need

Every business requires some basic equipment to operate. At the very least, you will need a reliable computer with a high-speed internet connection. While everything you need to create and manage your Etsy® shop is online and accessible using your favorite web browser, you'll also likely need specialized software to handle word processing, spreadsheets, inventory control, and bookkeeping, for example.

In addition, you'll likely need basic office equipment, such as a printer, scanner, fax machine, and telephone, as well as filing cabinets and a desk. As for office supplies,

► Protect Your Business with Proper Insurance

Consider investing in business and liability insurance right from the start. If you're running your business from home, your homeowner's or renter's insurance will not cover any damage or loss to any business equipment, supplies, or inventory. Plus, if something goes wrong with the product you sell, having liability insurance can help protect you financially against lawsuits from damage or injuries caused by your products.

Consult with any local insurance agent to discuss your needs as a small business or homebased business operator, and make sure you acquire ample insurance coverage. Insurance must be acquired *before* something bad happens and you need to file a claim, so plan accordingly.

business cards and company letterhead will be necessary, along with whatever other supplies are needed on a day-to-day basis.

As an online business operator who's selling products that need to be shipped, you'll need to designate an area that's stocked with all the appropriately sized boxes, packing tape, package scale, postage machine, and other shipping materials.

You may also find it useful to have a smartphone and tablet so you can respond to calls, email messages, and manage your social media accounts, for example, from virtually anywhere. Plus, you'll need whatever equipment and supplies are required to create whatever it is you'll be selling.

Learn from Experienced Etsy® Sellers

Etsy® offers a plethora of free online resources to help sellers become successful. These include:

> **aha!**
>
> Handmadeology [www.handmadeology.com/category/Etsy®-tips] is an online, independent source of Etsy®-related news, tips for sellers, and other useful information. Check out their list of Top 100 Home & Living Etsy® Sellers—2016 at www.handmadeology.com/top-100-home-living-Etsy-sellers-2016. By visiting some of the shops operated by these top sellers, you can study what makes them more successful than their competition.

- ▶ The *Seller Handbook* (www.Etsy.com/seller-handbook)
- ▶ Etsy®'s online Help Center (www.Etsy.com/help)
- ▶ Etsy®'s Community Forums (www.Etsy.com/forums)
- ▶ Etsy®'s Online Labs/instructional videos (www.Etsy.com/community/online-labs)

One of the best ways to become a successful Etsy® seller is to learn directly from the experiences of already successful Etsy® sellers. You can do this by reaching out to friends or family who have their own Etsy® shops, by contacting Etsy® sellers directly, and by reading the interviews featured in this book, starting with Dorene Nowatzke, the proprietor of an Etsy® shop called Columbia Fragrance Company.

Meet Dorene Nowatzke, Proprietor of Columbia Fragrance Company

Scented candles are popular, which is why there are countless retail chains, online shops, mass-market retailers, and individual artisans that create and sell them. Despite extensive competition, both online and in the real world, those who are able to somehow differentiate themselves in the marketplace, offer something unique, and/or define and target a niche audience with their products are typically able to achieve success selling online.

Dorene Nowatzke, who created a company called Columbia Fragrance (www.Etsy.com/shop/ColumbiaFragrance), is one example of this (shown in Figure 2–1).Through her Etsy® shop, she offers hand-poured candles and boutique home fragrances (in the form of melts, wickless candles for fragrance warmers, diffuser oils, and fragrance mists). One thing that differentiates her products from the competition is the unique selection of proprietary fragrances that she's developed.

"I have always been a creative person." recalls Nowatzke. "Over the years, I have done knitting, crochet, and other crafts. One year for Christmas, I decided I wanted to hand make candles for my coworkers. My husband asked if I had ever poured candles before, and I of course said, 'No, what does that matter?' I went to a local craft shop and bought a kit. I enjoyed doing this, kept pouring more and more candles, and wound up giving them away as presents for multiple holidays. It wasn't long, however, before I wound up with too many candles. I didn't know what to do with them all."

Combining her abundance of candle creations and some free time, at her friend's suggestion, she decided to start her own business in 2011. "At that point, I created at Etsy® shop, but it took a bit of time to get everything up and running. Back then, I was purely a hobbyist crafter who wanted to sell the large collection of candles I had created. Early

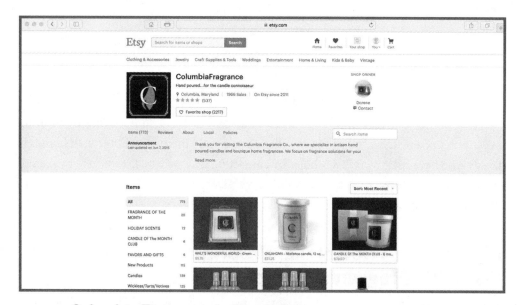

FIGURE 2–1: **Columbia Fragrance's Etsy® Shop**

on, I didn't put too much effort into the business aspect of the Etsy® shop. Eventually, someone I knew, who was also an Etsy® seller, asked me, 'Do you want to just continue making candles, or do you want to earn some money?' I stopped to think about what I was doing and how I was doing it. I determined that if I were going to run an Etsy® shop to sell my candles, I wanted to pursue it in a way that would allow me to make money," she adds.

Based on her newfound focus, Nowatzke tweaked her business model, changed her business' name to Columbia Fragrance, and began to focus on doing business-oriented tasks such as marketing and cost analysis. She states, "I needed to reduce my costs and figure out how to make the numbers work so I could pursue my passion and make money in the process. Back in 2011, Etsy® was known primarily as a crafter's marketplace. I knew of the service's existence and decided to look into it, along with other services. After reviewing what multiple platforms like Etsy® actually offered to sellers, I felt like Etsy® was the best platform for me."

Advice for Defining Your Audience and Identity

Knowing that she wanted to sell higher-end, hand-poured candles, Nowatzke needed to clearly define her target audience. "My target customers are predominately females who are in their early 20s to upper 40s, who like to spend some money gifting to themselves," she says. "My candles are not cheap. My products are something that customers are going to splurge a bit for, particularly if they're looking for a specific and unique scent.

"It was about three years ago that my Etsy® shop went from being a hobby to a more serious business. I had introduced a new scent, called 'Green Clover and Aloe.' One day, I had someone email me and ask if it was the same scent that's used within one of the popular Walt Disney World resorts. I responded that I didn't know, but I asked her to let me know once she received her order. She stated it was a perfect match. More and more customers responded that the scent reminded them of their stay at Walt Disney World. I ultimately wound up changing the name of the scent to "Walt's Wonderful World."

"More and more people found out about that one scent, and the product was picked up and featured within a popular blog. On the day the blog was published, I had an amazing number of sales. From that point, I developed relationships with blog writers who continue to this day to feature my products periodically. As a result of the success of 'Walt's Wonderful World,' I developed a selection of other Disney-inspired scents," added Nowatzke. "At this point, my target audience expanded to include fans of Disney who want to bring their Disney vacation memories home."

At the time Nowatzke first started using Etsy®, she thought of the service as being like an online farmer's market. "I thought it was a place that people with handcrafted goods sold their wares and where customers would come who were looking for those types of wares," says Nowatzke. "I quickly learned that Etsy® was not as homely as I thought. I discovered that, at the time, about 80 percent of the sellers came from that simple, homespun crafts market and about 20 percent of the sellers were operating more serious, profit-oriented businesses. Etsy® offers a seller's handbook, which offers good advice, but I initially thought that Etsy® was more of a community of sellers who were helping each other become successful. I really didn't discover that community, however."

She recalled that once she decided to launch an Etsy® business and take it seriously, she came up with the name for her business and then had it up and running within a week. She did very little upfront research and didn't bother to think about what her brand was going to be or how she should showcase that brand.

"I was impetuous," she explains. "There were a lot of starts, stops, and hiccups along the way. It wasn't until two years later, in 2013, that I rebranded my Etsy® shop, changed its name, and went from a more homespun crafty approach to more of an upscale boutique approach."

In terms of the "boutique approach," Nowatzke says that this included multiple changes in the way she operated her business. "My original company name was De-lites by Dory. I felt that was too homespun. It had a farmer's market feel, and that's an image I no longer wanted to convey. I did not want my shop to be a Country Candle shop that has scents like 'Apple Cinnamon Pie.' I wanted my products to be seen and appreciated for being more of an artisan candle or boutique candle that offered a more unique and contemporary scent. Not everyone likes a country candle, but they still want a home fragrance. This is how I decided to differentiate my candles."

It was also at this time that Nowatzke hired a designer to help her develop a company logo, product labels, and an overall brand for her business. Her goal was to change the way her products were visualized and perceived by her prospective customers. "Because I hired graphic designers who were my friends, I received discounted pricing, so this represented a minimal cost," she explains. "The time-consuming part was reshooting all my products with the new logo and branding. Once the changes were made, things started to happen pretty quickly. Within a few months, I experienced a 50 percent increase in sales, and this trend has continued."

For her product photography, Nowatzke does some of it herself but also works with a professional photographer. "For my core product shots that have a white background, I do those myself in-house. For the lifestyle product shots, I work with a photographer.

"Having really good product photography showcased throughout your Etsy® shop is imperative," she adds. "Without good shots, customers cannot get a good understanding of what they're buying. If a photo is out of focus or does not represent the product well, you won't sell products. As a seller, if you want to play with the big boys, your shop has to appear as professional looking as theirs, which means showcasing the highest quality photos possible."

For less than a $50 investment, Nowatzke purchased a light box which is used to take product photos. She also invested in a good-quality digital camera, although she also gets good results with the camera that's built into her smartphone.

Today, Columbia Fragrance is operated as a legitimate business venture, but it's not something that Nowatzke manages on a full-time basis. In the past year, her business has grown to the point where she's reached her current capacity to manage it because she also maintains a full-time job. "In the near future, I will need to either pursue this business on a full-time basis or hire employees to help run it. It took me about five years to reach this point," she says.

Finding the Right Approach

Nowatzke believes she took a very impulsive approach to launching her business early on. Looking back, if she were to do this again, knowing what she knows now, the advice she'd offer is simply, "slow down."

She explains, "I would take up to six months, if needed, to clearly define my product, define my brand, and pinpoint my target customers. I would also refine my product and acquire professional-quality product photos right from the start. I have learned that planning and research are essential."

Today, Nowatzke has learned how to multitask so she's able to make her candles and operate her business simultaneously. For example, while wax is melting or cooling, she can pre-process new orders or package finished items for shipping. "Creating and selling hand-poured candles really allows me to maximize my time. These days, I create candles three to four times per week, and the majority of my time is spent processing and shipping orders, as well as doing the other required back-office type of work," she adds.

One way Nowatzke has differentiated her products and added to their perceived value is by focusing a lot of time, research, and effort perfecting a customer's unboxing experience. Knowing that many of her customers are buying her candles as a gift to themselves, she ships all orders nicely packaged in a way that involves an unboxing experience that replicates the customer unwrapping a gift. Her goal is to make the customer feel special each and every time they receive and open their order. These activities fall into what she refers to as offering a "boutique shopping experience" for her customers, which is how she's now branded her business.

To ensure her candles remain unique and special, Nowatzke continuously invests time doing research about current fragrance trends. "If my research shows that people want water-related scents, I introduce rain-inspired fragrances, for example. I also try to be a trendsetter by offering a new twist to certain scents or products. To help generate repeat business, I formed a successful customer loyalty club and reward my customers based on how much they spend. For example, for every $100 someone spends, they receive a $10 gift certificate toward a future purchase. I want my customers to come back.

"Because my products are consumables, each time someone needs a new candle, I want them to come back to my Etsy® shop to explore what new seasonal scents I am offering or to replenish their supply of candles that feature the scents they already love," she adds. "With each order, I include a packing slip, business card, and loyalty club card, and I place all of this in a nice envelope as an upscale touch."

Her passion for candle making involves Nowatzke spending a lot of time developing and experimenting with new scents as well as candle colors. "The appearance of the product is as important as its scent. Because of my research and reputation, any time I put out a new product, my existing customers are willing to try it because they trust me. I release new scents and products every season, which keeps my inventory and selection fresh. I also release special scents for the holidays and special scents that cater to my Disney fans.

"At the same time I release new products, I am always reevaluating my product line and getting rid of products that are not selling. At least once per year, I get rid of the bottom 10 percent of items that are not selling well, based on sales. I do not allow my personal attachment to a fragrance or product to hinder this. I always have the option to relaunch a scent or product later. I try really hard to establish a balance between new products and getting rid of poorly selling products. Plus, I occasionally release specific scents or items for a very limited time," says Nowatzke.

For the people who just enjoy crafting and choose to sell their creations on Etsy® as a hobby, Nowatzke believes this is definitely a viable option. However, for the sellers who want to make money from their Etsy® shop, she discovered that taking a serious business approach and doing business tasks like a cost analysis, will help ensure that whatever is being sold earns a profit based on the cost of materials and the artisan's time investment that's needed to make the product.

"Even for sellers that opt to charge higher prices for premium goods, they still need to price their products competitively. However, as long as you can justify what you opt to charge, never be afraid to raise your prices. Potential customers will respect your pricing and be willing to pay a fair market price for a top quality, handmade product," adds Nowatzke.

Additional advice she offers to first-time sellers is that they should properly stock their Etsy® shop with a selection of products. "Etsy® is a virtual mall. If within your shop you only have three things, people might not visit your shop to see what you're offering. If your shop is visually attractive and offers a selection of products, you're more apt to draw customers in. At any given time, my Etsy® shop has at least 100 products available. Also, when populating your shop using Etsy®'s tools, use all of the categories that you can to make it easier for potential customers to find you. Focus on search engine optimization when choosing your keywords and tags, and when writing your product titles, as well as your product descriptions. What you say in the first paragraph or first sentence or two of every product listing is important for drawing in a potential customer and getting their attention," she says.

Using unique and creative product and scent names is all part of Nowatzke's branding efforts. "I try to create product and scent names that are clever. This is an important extension of my brand. Sometimes, scent or product names somehow relate to how I think or feel when using the candle. Other times, it somehow describes the scent, with the goal of kindling someone's scent memory.

"In other words, they think of a scent and remember something meaningful or special from their past. The Disney fans love the Disney-inspired scents because they remind them of a happy time and a happy vacation that they experienced with their friend or family, for example. Until they create technology that allows people to smell a candle while shopping online, I need to rely on creative scent and product names to convey what my scents offer," says Nowatzke.

Staying Visible Means Staying Relevant

Outside of using the search engine optimization (SEO) and marketing tools offered by the Etsy® platform, Nowatzke spends several hours per week managing her company's Facebook page as well as doing direct email marketing to her existing customers. "I am a big fan of email marketing, and it is a very powerful business tool, if used correctly. I use MailChimp to manage my email marketing," she adds.

Using email, she contacts her customers and people who have signed up for her email list just one time per week or once every two weeks. This includes sending out a monthly enewsletter. On other weeks, she'll remind people about her loyalty club, offer tips for using her products, or send out an email promoting new scents or products.

"I try to target holidays or special days with flash sales that I promote through Facebook or email. For example, on 'National Raspberry Ice Cream Day,' I do a flash sale on all raspberry scented products. I do research about quirky holidays and then create sales around them throughout the year. Doing this allows me to showcase fragrances that I might not have promoted in a while," explains Nowatzke.

Without hesitation, Nowatzke describes Etsy® as the "primary online marketplace for artisans." She concludes, "If you're going to sell your crafts or handmade products online, Etsy® is the place you should be to do this. Yes, there's a lot of competition, but I am a firm believer that competition forces you to improve yourself, your business approach, and your products. Try to learn what you can from your competition. That being said, I have found Etsy® to be a very secure place to sell.

"As a seller, positive ratings and reviews from customers are very important. When a customer leaves a review saying that a scent smells exactly as they thought it should smell like, based on its name or product description, that type of feedback helps my reputation a lot. Positive reviews make customers feel more confident placing an order for an item they cannot smell for themselves prior to making a purchase. When a customer leaves a review, I always send them a thank-you note for their opinion. I also cut and paste text reviews directly into my product descriptions if a review helps to describe a particular fragrance, for example.

"To be successful, a seller really needs to be aware of what their brand represents, and who their target customer is. Sellers who run an Etsy® shop need to find creative ways to differentiate themselves from their competition. I have tried purchasing paid ads on Etsy® to promote my shop and products, and they did work. Due to demand for my products, paid advertising is not something I have had to do too often.

"Six years ago, I never would have thought I'd be where I am today in terms of the success of Columbia Fragrance. I am very grateful to my customers. I am so proud that I have been able to see my business grow and have learned so much during each step of this journey. In fact, I never stop learning."

Additional Thoughts

Even if you're launching an Etsy® shop to sell products you create as part of what you define as your hobby, as soon as your shop goes online, in reality, you will be operating a legitimate small business. Thus, it's important that you always handle yourself in a professional manner as you juggle the various responsibilities that operating a small business entails. Now that you have a general idea about what'll be required of you, let's focus a bit on what launching your business might cost. That's the focus of the next chapter.

Calculating Your Costs and Setting Your Prices

Prior to reading this book, you probably already had some idea about what it is you want to sell on Etsy®. Before going through the effort of setting up your shop and opening for business, invest some time, research, and effort into five things:

1. Determine what exactly you want to sell.

2. Calculate how much money you'll need to invest in equipment and supplies to get started.

3. Develop relationships with suppliers, manufacturers, and other services you will need to create and package your product(s).

4. Determine how much you'll sell your product(s) for, taking into account all the costs associated with creating/manufacturing your items, how much you want/need to be paid for your time, your business operation expenses and overhead, and how much profit you want to earn per item sold.

5. Start building and managing your product inventory.

Whether you opt to sell your items through your Etsy® shop, craft fairs, retail shops, or your own website, it's important to first figure out if there is a demand for your product(s) from a large enough group of people. This will help you forecast whether or not your business will be profitable. After calculating all of your expenses, you should be able to create, market, and sell your product(s) at a price point that customers are willing to pay and that's competitive with your competition in the existing marketplace.

Define Your Product Offering

Based on your skill set and interests, chances are you already have a good idea about what you want to create and sell online through your Etsy® shop. Now it is time to define your initial product offerings. What are the main items you plan to sell, and what colors, designs, sizes, and other related options will you offer to your customers?

Once you figure this out for your main product(s), start brainstorming about additional but related products you can simultaneously offer. For example, if you plan to knit sweaters, consider offering matching hats, mittens, and scarves to be sold separately. If you plan to sell handcrafted silver or gold necklaces, consider offering matching earrings and/or bracelets to give your customers additional optionsand perhaps generate larger sales when your customers purchase multiple items as bundles.

Based on the size, design, and color options you plan to offer for each product, think about what your inventory requirements will be, how long it will take you

tip

If you plan to offer multiple products that target a vastly different audience, consider setting up separate Etsy® shops, with each one focusing on just one target audience. Then within each shop, only offer related items you know will be of direct interest to that audience.

to create each item, and how you'll showcase and promote each option within your Etsy® shop. For example, if you handcraft a silver bracelet but also sell a version in 24k gold with a slightly different design, that would be considered a separate product. However, if you offer the same product in three different sizes (i.e., small, medium, and large), that would be a customer-selectable option offered within each single product listing on Etsy®.

Use the worksheet shown in Figure 3–1 to help you define what products you'll offer within your Etsy® shop. Each item that will ultimately be a separate product listing within your Etsy® shop should be listed separately.

Product Worksheet

Product Name	Product Description	Size Options to be Offered	Color Options to be Offered	Customizations to be Offered
Star Design Bracelet	Bracelet featuring star design	S, M, L, XL, XXL	Silver	N/A
Moon Design Bracelet	Bracelet featuring moon design	S, M, L, XL, XXL	Gold or Silver	N/A

FIGURE 3–1: **Product Worksheet**
Define each of your products.

As you summarize each of the products, think about your target customers and consider what additional, but related, products they might want. Also consider what their motivation is for buying your product(s) and what potential objections or concerns they might have that might keep them from placing an order.

Define Your Audience

As you determine who your primary target audience will be for your Etsy® shop and your product offerings, define that niche audience as narrowly and clearly as possible. How you define your audience can be based on a wide range of factors, or any combination of factors, including the following:

- ▶ Age
- ▶ Club or association memberships
- ▶ Education level
- ▶ Gender
- ▶ Geographic location
- ▶ Hobbies
- ▶ Income
- ▶ Interests
- ▶ Marital status
- ▶ Occupation
- ▶ Religion
- ▶ Residence type (house, apartment, condo, etc.)
- ▶ Sexual orientation
- ▶ Social media usage
- ▶ Spending habits
- ▶ Vehicle make and model that they drive
- ▶ Weight or other physical attributes
- ▶ Where and when they travel
- ▶ Where they work
- ▶ Any other factors you can clearly define

tip

According to Etsy®, two large groups of buyers on Etsy® are women who are recently engaged and planning their wedding, as well as women who are pregnant and expecting a child. Thus, these people are shopping for wedding-related items or unique (handmade) baby products for themselves or to give as gifts.

For example, you may determine that your target audience is comprised of women between the ages of 18 and 34, who live in a major city, earn at least $50,000 per year, and need to dress up for work each day, so they like to accessorize their outfits with handcrafted jewelry. Or, perhaps your primary target audience is comprised of women ages 24 to 34 who are engaged and planning their wedding.

Using this list, as well as any other factors you deem appropriate, write out one or two sentences that clearly define the primary target audience for your product(s). Then, repeat this process to define exactly who would comprise a secondary target audience for your product(s).

Ultimately, you'll want to invest most of your marketing and advertising resources to reach your core target audience, but you can run separate advertising or marketing campaigns that specifically target your secondary audiences as well.

The more narrowly and clearly you define your target market, the more effective your ad campaigns will be, especially if you opt to use paid online advertising options such as Facebook or Google AdWords.

Determine What Equipment You Need

When it comes to creating, making, or manufacturing whatever it is you'll be selling, you will have the following four primary categories of costs associated with it:

1. *Tools.* This is the equipment that needs to be purchased once and that you will use repeatedly to create your products. For example, if you'll be knitting and selling handmade sweaters, your tools will include an assortment of knitting needles and maybe a sewing machine. If you need to acquire expensive tools or machinery, consider buying this equipment used. Then, using profits you earn down the road, you can always upgrade your tools and equipment later.

2. *Supplies/Materials.* These are the raw materials required to create your products that you will continuously need to replenish. Being able to obtain your supplies and materials for the lowest price possible will definitely help your business become profitable faster and stay profitable in the future. This will require you to seek out and negotiate the best deals possible from wholesalers, distributors, suppliers, and/or manufacturers. If you'll be knitting and selling handmade sweaters, your supplies include wool, buttons, and/or zippers, for example.

stat fact

Statistics show that the majority of Etsy® buyers are women who tend to find products using Etsy®'s built-in search field. Therefore, your shop should focus on this demographic and utilize Etsy®'s SEO tools. Keep in mind, however, that many Etsy® shops successfully cater to a male demographic. However, you may find it necessary to actively drive more of your own traffic to your shop by using paid ads or social media, for example, if your target audience does not closely fit those who already do some of their shopping on Etsy®.com.

3. *Packaging.* This includes the additional materials needed to package your product(s) so they're ready to showcase, sell, and ship to customers.

4. *Shipping.* This includes the cost of all shipping materials, including boxes, labels, stuffing, packing tape, postage, and anything else required to fulfill an order and ship your product(s) to your customers.

Choose the Right Materials and Supplies

Once you have determined exactly what product(s) you plan to create, build, make, or manufacture, carefully evaluate your step-by-step process for creating each product. Make a list of the tools and equipment you already have and what additional tools and equipment you need to purchase. The money needed to make these initial equipment/tool purchases will become part of the startup costs for your business.

Next, focus on establishing a comprehensive list of the materials and supplies you need to create your product(s). This will help you determine your cost of goods sold. You'll want to determine how much of each item you need to create a single product that you'll be selling. This will ultimately allow you to determine your raw materials cost for each item you create. Use Figure 3–2 on page 43 to help you gather the supply/material information you need.

tip

Most crafters, artisans, and artists acquire their supplies and materials from a local crafts shop, such as Jo-Ann shops (www.joann.com) or Michaels (www.michaels.com); or they shop from an online retailer and pay retail prices for their tool and supply purchases. As a small-business operator, once you acquire a tax identification number and establish yourself as a business entity, you should seek out wholesale sellers or distributors for your tools, supplies, and materials and pay wholesale prices when you purchase what you need in quantity. This typically allows you to save 30 to 50 percent (compared to retail prices).

When it comes to calculating costs, after determining your quantity needs for each raw material needed to create your product(s), it will likely be necessary to source some wholesalers or distributors so you can acquire what you need in bulk and pay wholesale prices.

Etsy® offers a variety of online tools designed to help sellers find and partner with manufacturers related to tools, supplies, and raw materials needed to create apparel and textiles, machining and fabrication, jewelry and metalsmithing, as well as printing. To explore these tools, discover valuable resources, as well as find leads for reputable manufacturers,

Product to be Manufactured/Created and Sold:_____

Supply/Material Description	Product/Item/Part Number (UPC Code)	Quantity Needed to Create One Finished Product	Wholesale Material Cost Per Finished Product

FIGURE 3–2: **Supplies/Materials List**

wholesalers, distributors, and suppliers, visit: www.Etsy.com/manufacturing.

Once you pinpoint a supplier, wholesaler, or manufacturer that sells exactly what you need, set up an account with that company or open a line of credit with each supplier. What you'll discover is that the wholesale discount you receive when buying items in bulk will be determined by the quantity of each item you purchase. The more you purchase per order, the lower your cost will be.

Of course, before committing to working with a supplier, wholesaler, or manufacturer,

tip

The easiest way to find a wholesaler or distributor is to type what you're looking for into an internet search engine, such as Yahoo! or Google. For example, if you need to purchase wool, type the search phrase, "wool wholesaler" or "yarn wholesaler." When possible, you might consider buying your supplies/materials directly from the manufacturer, which may be located overseas.

you always want to discuss with them your immediate and long-term needs. Request samples to make sure the quality is good, and make sure that you'll be able to obtain the quantity of each item you need within the desired time frame. This will require you to ask questions. Don't just make decisions based on who offers you the lowest prices. After all, if you use poor quality materials to create your product, this will directly correlate with the quality of your finished product(s).

Once you figure out your raw material/supply cost to create each product you will be selling, this cost will be used to help you formulate the wholesale and retail price that you'll ultimately sell your product(s) for.

Focus on Product Packaging

In many situations, simply creating an awesome product is not enough to be successful as an Etsy® seller or online business operator. You may also want or need to develop packaging for the product. Your product packaging needs will be dictated by the type of product you're selling, as well as the image you want to convey to your customers. Typically, you want the product name, your company logo, and related information about the product to appear somewhere on your packaging, and you want the packaging to be visually attention-getting and appealing to your target customers in a way that best depicts your brand.

Determine what additional materials and supplies are needed to create the product packaging for each of the items you plan to sell, and calculate the cost associated with the packaging. Your packaging costs need to be added to your cost of goods.

Figure Out Your Shipping Requirements

Once one of your items is manufactured, built, created, or made and has been placed within its packaging, you

aha!

To help you better navigate your way through the manufacturing processes, as well as learn the lingo needed to negotiate properly with manufacturers, wholesalers, distributors, and/or suppliers, Etsy® offers the Etsy® Manufacturing Glossary, which is a free, downloadable document that can be found online at: http://extfiles.Etsy®.com/mfg/Etsy®Manufacturing-Glossary.pdf.

tip

Etsy® offers an interactive Excel worksheet template that you can use to calculate your cost of goods sold. To download this free template, visit: http://extfiles.Etsy®.com/worksheets/Cost%20of%20Goods%20Sold%20Worksheet%202.xls.

▶ Never Rely on Just One Supplier

When seeking out wholesalers, suppliers, or manufacturers, always find at least two or three different sources for each item you need. Then, if one supplier runs out of the item, discontinues the item, or goes out of business, you can immediately turn to your backup supplier(s) to ensure you always have a source for the materials/supplies you require so you are able to continue to create, build, make, or manufacture your products.

By relying on just one supplier, you could find yourself unable to fill your orders and maintain your inventory if there are ever unforeseen hangups. This could potentially force you out of business or cause major delays that your customers will not appreciate.

Another drawback to relying on one supplier is that if that company dramatically raises their prices for the materials you need, your product manufacturing costs could skyrocket. As a result, your profit margin will diminish. It could become impossible for you to generate any profit whatsoever once you cover your cost of goods sold and other expenses.

When it comes to the manufacturing process for your product(s), one of the biggest challenges will be ensuring that you always have an ample supply of all materials and supplies you need on hand. Keep in mind that in some cases, one or more of your materials or supplies may need to be shipped from overseas, so it could take extra days or weeks to receive them once an order is placed. Thus, you will continuously need to predict your needs and place your orders accordingly, based on how quickly each supplier can fulfill your orders.

now need to figure out what's required to safely ship that item to your customers. Figure out what size shipping box you will need, and what stuffing will be placed in the box to prevent the product from damage, and then figure out what additional shipping supplies are required, such as a shipping label and packing tape.

Next, determine the best options for shipping your product. You may discover the most cost-effective and efficient shipping method is the U.S. Post Office's (USPS) Priority Mail service because fixed-rate boxes are offered in a variety of sizes for free. However, based on the size and weight

aha!

When determining your shipping methods and the options you'll offer to your customers, be sure to build in the extra costs for insurance and package tracking. Based on the value of the items you'll be shipping, you may also want to require a signature on delivery. These services often cost extra but are absolutely necessary.

of the packages you'll be shipping, as well as the quantity of packages you'll be shipping out each day, you may find that using UPS, FedEx, or another courier is more efficient and economical.

UPS, FedEx, and other couriers offer a variety of shipping options at different price points. For example, there's overnight, second-day, third-day, and ground shipping options, which you may want to offer to your customers. In most cases, your customers will expect, or at least desire, that ground shipping and related handling fees be included in the retail price of your product, although most consumers are accustomed to having shipping and handling fees added to their order's subtotal.

You might opt to offer free ground shipping but charge extra for overnight or second-day shipping. If a customer requests Priority Mail shipping, for example, they know that, in most cases, this means the shipping time will be two days. Thus, it's important that you promptly fill and ship the order on the same day a customer places it or within the reasonable time frame that you promise.

tip

The *Etsy® Seller Handbook* offers multiple articles related to packaging and shipping items to your customers and explains how to set up your Etsy® shop to offer a variety of shipping options for your customers, based on the size, weight, and value of the product(s) you'll be shipping. For more information visit: www. Etsy.com/seller-handbook/category/shipping.

If your manufacturing time is two to three weeks for made-to-order products, make sure the customer knows before they place their order. Then they need to add additional time to receive their order, based on the shipping method that's selected.

Ultimately, you'll probably want to offer a variety of shipping options to your customers and, when possible (based on what you're selling), be able to fill orders and ship them out within 24 hours after each order is received.

Based on the shipping options you decide to offer, the USPS, UPS, FedEx, and most other couriers offer a variety of online, software, and/or mobile app tools that allow you to prepare and pay for shipments, easily request a package pickup, and at the same time keep track of your shipping-related expenses, track packages, and, if necessary, process an insurance claim.

Calculate and Set Your Product's Retail Price

So far, this chapter has helped you calculate your one-time tool/equipment costs, your materials/supply costs, as well as your packaging and shipping costs. Knowing this information will help you set the wholesale and retail prices for whatever it is you'll be selling.

However, you'll also want to add in your additional costs of doing business—your overhead costs—such as your ongoing marketing and advertising expenses, insurance costs, and business operating costs (including your phone service, internet service, as well as office equipment and supplies).

Next, you need to determine how much you want to be paid for your time. Setting your "hourly rate" will be based on several factors, including:

tip

Etsy® offers a free Microsoft Excel template that will help you calculate and track your ongoing business expenses. To download this free template, visit: http://bit.ly/1SIRRA5.

▶ What you're selling
▶ The uniqueness of your skill or expertise as an artist, crafter, or artisan
▶ How long it takes to create the product/item
▶ Your own sense of self-worth from a financial standpoint
▶ The affluence of your target audience and how much they're willing to pay

Based on these factors, you may set your own hourly wage to be equal to your state's minimum wage, or you could opt to pay yourself $10, $20, or more per hour. This wage will need to be calculated into the wholesale and retail price of your product.

The widely accepted formula for setting the wholesale and retail price for what you'll be selling can be calculated by following these steps:

1. Calculate the cost of your materials/supplies per item you will be selling. For this example, let's say your materials/supplies cost is $10 per item.

2. Amortize the fixed tool costs and overhead costs for your business and calculate what percentage needs to be covered per item you will be selling. For this example, let's say this figure comes out to $15 per item. (Overhead costs include your Etsy® listing fees, Etsy® sales commissions, PayPal fees, advertising, office supplies, internet service fees, etc.)

3. Figure out how long it takes you to make each item. Then calculate the cost of your time, based on the hourly wage you set for yourself. For example, if each item takes you exactly two hours of time to create and you opt to pay yourself $10.00 per hour, the cost of your time per item is $20.

4. How much profit per item do you want/need to earn to keep your business afloat and stay happy? This profit markup amount should be realistic and acceptable by your customers. For this example, let's say it's $5 per item. Determine how much

you want to earn per week, month, quarter, or annually. This will help you measure your success and provide you with the financial resources needed to continue operating and ultimately expand your business.

Add together the cost per item for steps one, two, three, and four. For this example, you'd add together $10 + $15 + $20 + $5, which is $50. This is your cost to create each item. To calculate your wholesale price, double your cost. For this example, your wholesale price would be $100.

tip

You might decide to reinvest profits into your business to expand, buy new tools/equipment, or boost your advertising efforts.

To calculate your retail price (what you will sell your item for within your Etsy®-based shop to individual customers), double your wholesale price. Thus, for this example, your retail price would be $200. If you plan to include shipping and handling fees and offer this for free to your customers, add this cost to your retail price. Otherwise, list the shipping and handling fee separately and have Etsy® add this to the customer's order subtotal when an order is placed. Likewise, your Etsy® shop can also be set up to calculate and charge sales tax, if applicable. Sales tax does not need to be built into your retail prices.

Displayed more simply, here's what the formulas looks like:

▶ Raw Material Cost + Labor Wages + Expenses + Desired Profit = Wholesale Price
▶ Wholesale Price x 2 = Retail Price

Depending on what you're selling, demand for your product(s), your competition's pricing, and other related factors, you may need to adjust the formula to calculate your retail pricing. Based on what you determine (through research and getting to know your target customers) what you're able to charge, you may need to somehow reduce your manufacturing costs, spend less money on paid advertising, or lower your hourly wage a bit to stay competitive.

However, if you're offering something that's unique, rare, or that utilizes a specific skill or talent that few other people have, you'll likely be able to charge a premium for your product(s), in which case you can increase your hourly wage, for example.

As a business operator, you'll constantly need to re-evaluate your costs and determine ways to lower them while brainstorming ways to enhance the quality and/or perceived value of your product(s), which could allow you to increase your prices.

Ultimately, you will want to price your products fairly and competitively and in a way that allows you to generate at least a meager profit. Of course, you must also be able to negotiate the lowest prices possible for your tools, supplies, and materials and keep your other costs as low as possible, as this too will impact profitability for your business venture.

You can set any price for your items on Etsy®. However, if you want customers to buy what you're selling, they need to believe your products are actually worth the price you're charging. Ask yourself why a buyer should consider purchasing your product instead of the competition's similar product.

Perhaps the answer is that you use better materials and the overall product quality is much higher. Maybe your product showcases more intricate or complex craftsmanship, or it offers additional features or functions that the competition's products do not offer.

Whatever it is that is unique or special about your product and that can make it stand out from the competition must be detailed clearly within your product descriptions and, when applicable, showcased within your product photos. If you are able to increase the perceived value of your product, the customer won't hesitate to spend a bit more for it. Thus, it becomes your job as a seller to promote your products in a way that clearly

tip

To help you calculate the ideal price for whatever it is you'll be selling, Etsy® offers a free, downloadable, "How to Price Like a Pro" Microsoft Excel worksheet, which you'll find online at: http://Etsy®.me/1h6YUf0.

► When Dealing with Heavy Competition, Pay Even Closer Attention to Your Profit Margin

If you're selling a product on Etsy® (or elsewhere) that's very common and you have a lot of competition, chances are you'll wind up in a price war and will need to undercut your competition to attract the attention of customers. Especially in a business that involves you investing your own time and effort into creating/manufacturing your own products, this is not a good situation to be in.

Your chances of achieving success and profitability increase dramatically if you're able to separate yourself from your competition by offering something that's unique, higher quality, or that your customers will be willing to pay extra for.

Being in a price war with your competition will result in you earning much lower profits and could ultimately lead to you operating your business at a loss, with little or no chance of ever earning a profit.

and prominently showcases what makes it special and what differentiates it from the competition.

Never assume that your customers will automatically see what's unique or special about your products or that the differentiating factors between your products and what the competition offers are obvious. Figure out what makes your products special, and promote this within your Etsy® shop, within your product listings, within your product photography, and when telling your seller/company story, for example.

Start Building Your Inventory in Preparation for Opening Your Business

Assuming you won't be custom manufacturing each product, you'll want to build up an initial inventory prior to opening your Etsy® shop. That way, you'll be able to fill an order to your customers on the same day they trickle in (or within 24 hours of when you receive them).

Being able to fill orders promptly will help you earn high ratings and favorable reviews from your initial customers, which will prove extremely valuable when it comes to enhancing your credibility as a seller and boosting your business's online reputation. As you'll discover from the next chapter, every Etsy® shop displays when it was established, how many orders the seller has received to date, as well as the seller's ratings and reviews. Especially if it's obvious that you're a new seller on Etsy® and that you've had just a few previous orders, being able to showcase the highest possible ratings and reviews from your initial customers becomes that much more important.

tip

As you begin creating your initial inventory, seek out ways you can streamline the manufacturing process, reduce your materials/supplies cost, and improve on the product so it becomes more attractive, valuable, or useful to your customers. During this time, you may also come up with ways to improve or modify the product, brainstorm ideas for additional products or come up with product add-ons that your customers will be interested in.

Consider Offering Product Bundles

Bundling products is a creative way to add perceived value to your products. If you have two, three, or four related items, in addition to selling them separately, also offer them as a discounted bundle. For example, if you sell sweaters, matching mittens, and matching scarves separately, add an additional product listing to your Etsy® shop that offers these three items together at a discounted price (say, 20 percent off, assuming this allows you to generate a profit). Your added cost to create a new product listing is a mere $0.20, so why not give product bundling a try?

Meet Kristen Berry, Proprietor of Miss Design Berry

Kristen Berry studied design in school and went on to land a job right out of college at a New York City advertising agency, where she worked as an art director. During her spare time, she started doing some freelance design work and ultimately learned about Etsy® as a way to potentially showcase and sell her work.

"I started my Etsy® business as a way to earn extra money creating logos and graphic designs for people," explains Berry. "Ultimately, I fell into a wedding niche and began focusing on wedding-related graphic design, creating invitations, engagement announcements, and other wedding-related graphics and artwork. Over the next four years, I slowly grew my online business on Etsy® and ultimately left my full time job in 2015 to pursue running my Etsy®-based business on a full-time basis."

Focusing on the wedding niche, Miss Design Berry (www.Etsy.com/shop/MissDesign BerryInc) offers personalized guest books, ornaments, wedding books, invitations, holiday cards, custom wrapping paper, and other items that showcase original wedding or holiday-themed artwork. Her Etsy® business has earned well over 2,500 five-star ratings and reviews and has generated more than 12,500 sales since it was established.

Since transforming Miss Design Berry (shown in Figure 3–3, page 52) into a full-time job, Kristen Berry has brought on one equity-holding business partner and has more than a dozen people working for her on a part-time basis. "We do maintain our own website [www.MissDesignBerry.com]; however, we maintain a strong presence on Etsy®," says Berry.

She adds, "When I first decided to build my online business using the Etsy® platform, I discovered that becoming proficient using the service as a seller requires a bit of a learning curve. I spent a lot of time visiting the Etsy® forums and discovered insights from lots of other Etsy® sellers as I was creating my shop. There is a skill involved with creating product listings on Etsy®, for example, that will ultimately be seen by and attract the audience that you need to target for your products."

Although there are other services online that offer similar functionality to Etsy®, Berry recalls that she chose Etsy® because it was the service she had heard the most about. "Over the years, I have looked at other services and have even tried a few of them, but I am most

FIGURE 3–3: **The Miss Design Berry Storefront on Etsy®**

impressed with the features, functions, and tools that Etsy® offers to its sellers. I also like Etsy® because it has a vast, dedicated, and ever-growing customer base. I have looked into working with Amazon Handmade, but for some reason, I have not been approved as a seller on that service," states Berry.

Initially, Berry didn't focus her graphic design work on the wedding niche and instead offered services like custom logo design through her Etsy® shop. She ultimately discovered that wedding-related items are one of Etsy®'s biggest markets and began to focus her efforts on creating customized products that catered to this already established customer base. "People are always getting married and are willing to spend money on quality products for their wedding, she adds. "I have found that creating wedding-related graphics offers very satisfying work for me from a creative standpoint as well."

When people first open an Etsy® shop, they expect to begin receiving sales almost immediately. This expectation is not realistic. "I went into this with few expectations and never would have guessed that within two years, this online-based business would become a full-time and profitable career for me. If anything, Etsy® has blown my initial expectations out of the water. Initially, I invested a few days to design and build my Etsy® shop, which I continue to fine-tune. Being a graphic designer, I was easily able to create my own professional-looking logo and banner, which I believe are key elements of an Etsy® shop," says Berry.

"One piece of advice I can offer to new Etsy® sellers is that when they're creating their shop, fill in every field that requests information. Don't leave anything blank. Provide a logo, banner, business description, profile, profile image, detailed item descriptions, professional-looking photos, as well as anything else the service asks for as you're building your shop. If a seller has neglected to supply an important piece of requested information, this can be detrimental to attracting customers and building their trust. It also shows you're not fully invested in your own business."

"The branding, imaging, color scheme, logo, photographs, and artwork you use to establish your business on Etsy® should nicely reflect you and your business and directly appeal to your target audience. It may take you some time to develop your brand identity, and as you're getting started, it's important that you maintain patience. It was at least one full month between the time I first launched my Etsy® shop and when I received my first order," she recalls. "Even for the first year, I'd receive sales sporadically, maybe just one or two per week. Over time, the frequency and regularity of new orders increased."

As recently as two years ago, Berry generated about $50,000 in sales through her Etsy® shop. One year ago, she generated $175,000 in sales and projected that in 2016 she'd generate more than $500,000 in sales. "Expect your shop to grow incrementally, she says. "However, there is a direct correlation between the amount of time you invest into your business and the amount of sales you'll generate from it. If you treat your Etsy® business as a hobby, you'll earn a hobby-size income. If you treat it like a full-time business, you could earn a respectable income from it. There is a direct correlation between your effort and the results you achieve."

When you're setting up your Etsy® shop, Berry recommends that you become fully conscious of how potential customers will view your online presence as well as what you're selling. "It's essential that you respond to customer inquiries immediately, advises Berry. "Don't wait a day or two, for example.

For me, the biggest challenge setting up my Etsy® shop was to overcome the limitations Etsy® has when creating your product listings. You need to utilize their format in a way that best showcases whatever it is you'll be selling. Invest whatever time is needed to become familiar with the tools available to you as a seller, and then discover how to work with those tools to best reach your target audience by showcasing what you're selling in the most effective and compelling way possible," says Berry.

These days, Berry spends 75 percent of her time handling the administrative responsibilities related to managing her Etsy® shop and the business as a whole. The other 25 percent of her time is spent doing design work. Most of her effort is spent running the business and juggling the different roles she needs to manage to maintain the business's growth and success. "I would love to spend more time doing design and creative work, but I am very pleased with how the business has grown," adds Berry.

To continuously build her business, Berry utilized paid online advertising on Pinterest, Instagram, and Facebook, as well as on several prominent wedding blogs. Berry explains, "We also do occasional online ad campaigns using other services, like Google AdWords. Plus, we participate in vendor wedding trade shows, but for my business, those don't generate the same return as online advertising. Pinterest has an established member base of women who are getting engaged or who are recently engaged and who use the service as a wedding planning tool. This allows me to reach our target audience rather easily through paid advertising. Instagram is also a very visual platform, which is conducive to allowing us to showcase our work, which is very visual."

Outside of paid advertising, Miss Berry Design does maintain a presence on the various social media services and encourages customer interaction through these services. However, Berry personally prefers to communicate with prospective and existing customers through direct email.

When it comes to setting her pricing on Etsy®, Berry never paid too much attention to what her competition online or in the real world was doing. Instead, she calculated how long it would take her to produce something, what the materials cost would be, and how much she wanted to be paid for her time. "Our prices tend to be higher than what our competition on Etsy® charges for similar products, but we really focus on offering superior customer service and top-quality products. I have found that many Etsy® sellers underprice whatever they're selling and wind up earning about $2 per hour. I put a value on my time and set my prices accordingly," she adds.

In terms of competition, Miss Design Berry has been forced to hire a lawyer to protect its trademarks and copyrights related to designs that have been stolen or blatantly copied. When she discovers a competitor who has stolen or copied one of her designs, she begins by contacting that person or company directly. When necessary, she turns the situation over to her attorney, although she has discovered that Etsy® offers tools for sellers who feel that their intellectual properties have been infringed.

"If I discover a situation that needs to be addressed, I contact the individual or company directly. If that doesn't result in an adequate solution, I file a report with Etsy® via email. Only rarely do I ultimately need to work with my attorney to protect my trademarks, copyrights, or intellectual properties that have been infringed, but at times, this does become necessary. Obviously, once you involve an attorney, that costs money. I use all of the resources at my disposal to protect my artwork and designs," says Berry. "I believe it is very important to be proactive in terms of protecting your work by filing the appropriate copyrights and trademarks, as applicable. This includes protecting your company name, slogan, and logo, as well as the work itself."

Because Miss Design Berry now outsources work to other artists and utilizes photographers, website designers, and other professionals, Berry says she's needed to become an expert negotiator. "One thing that many new Etsy® sellers don't realize is how much work you need to put into your business to make it successful. As a result, people become frustrated with the experience. You need to be patient, have confidence in your business and products, and maintain persistent efforts. Also, do adequate research to develop the business-oriented skills you will need to operate your particular business and then properly promote it," says Berry.

In terms of maintaining customer loyalty, Berry's policy is that as long as her customers are showing her proper respect, she will do whatever is necessary to make them 100 percent happy. "As soon as a customer becomes abusive or stops treating us with respect, then we will either turn down their work or complete the work as quickly as possible and move on. I absolutely love the flexibility that running my own business offers. Running Miss Design Berry is both emotionally and financially rewarding for me. I love my job, and I work more hours per week than I should because I love what I am doing," she concludes.

Additional Thoughts

The key to operating any successful business is to focus on the money. It's essential that you keep close tabs on your manufacturing costs and all other expenses and then price your products accordingly to ensure you're able to earn a profit. At the same time, you of course need to be cognizant of what your competition is doing so you're able to remain competitive. Once you determine you have a great product to sell and establish a fair price for it, the next step is to establish yourself as a seller on Etsy® (and/or additional online selling platforms). That's the focus of the next chapter.

Establishing Yourself as an Etsy® Seller

O nce you've come up with the perfect product(s) to sell on Etsy®, and after doing some number crunching, hopefully you've determined that you could sustain a viable business by offering your product selection(s) to the target audience you've identified. The next step is to establish a presence on Etsy®.

As you'll discover later in the chapter, the actual steps to set up and open your Etsy® shop are relatively straightforward. However, developing your brand and drafting the content for your shop is what will take time, resources, and effort. Be sure to populate your shop in a way that targets your audience and allows you to best showcase the products you intend to sell.

Therefore, the first portion of this chapter is dedicated to the prep work you'll need to do. Most of the work involves some research and writing drafts of all text that will ultimately be showcased and incorporated within your shop. So, before you go online to create your shop, there are a variety of important tasks you'll want to complete first. These tasks include:

▶ *Explore Etsy® as a buyer.* Visit shops and assess what you like and don't like about the approach various sellers take. This will help identify who your key competition might be. Try Etsy®'s search field and enter keywords or phrases that relate to what you plan to sell and see what similar products are currently being offered.

▶ *Brainstorm a descriptive, attention-getting, and memorable name for your shop.* Keep in mind that Etsy® displays shop names (and establishes a shop's unique web-

▶ Learn What You Can by Studying the Approach Other Sellers Take

As you study the Etsy® shops you visit as a buyer, pay attention to the interesting ways various sellers showcase their overall brand. Study how sellers tell their story, describe their products, depict their products in photos, explain their return policies and guarantees, capitalize on their positive ratings and reviews, and justify their pricing.

Also, pay attention to the seller's use of color throughout their shop, as well as how the company's logo (if applicable) is displayed and utilized as a tool for establishing the company's brand.

When visiting various Etsy® shops as a buyer, if you don't believe you're part of a seller's target audience, pretend you are and focus on how well the content of each shop you visit caters to your wants, needs, concerns, and interests as a buyer.

Through your own research, discover what approaches you believe work well, what approaches you dislike, and think about ways you'll populate your own Etsy® shop with content that will capture the attention of your target audience and ultimately help you stand out from your competition.

site address) by removing spaces from company names that are comprised of two or more words. Because many potential customers will learn about your shop from Etsy®'s search option, one approach some sellers adopt is to create a company name that relates directly to what they're selling.

▶ *Create a logo for your company.* Once you've determined that your company name is available and does not violate anyone else's trademarks or copyrights, create a logo. This will be displayed prominently in your Etsy® shop, as well as in all your advertising, marketing, product packaging, and other materials that your customers and potential customers will see. This includes your letterhead, business cards, and invoices, for example.

▶ *Draft your product descriptions.* After determining exactly what you'll be selling and who you'll be selling to, start drafting your product descriptions. Use an easy-to-read and upbeat style because it's your text-based product descriptions that must capture the attention of potential customers and convince them to buy your product(s). Thus, you want each product description to explain exactly what the product is and what's special about it, and answer basic questions such as why does the customer need it and what sets it apart from the competition. Focus on unique features or functions, for example.

▶ *Take your product photos.* Every product listing should include at least several product photos that are crystal clear, showcase the detail of your product, and look professional.

▶ *Write your shop's story.* One of the important components of every Etsy® shop is the "About" section. It's here that you can use text, photos, or links to videos to tell your story, share your inspiration, explain your philosophy, and humanize your business. More often than not, it's your unique shop that will pique a potential customer's interest and help convince them to become a paying customer. Your story should also be written in a clear, concise, and upbeat style, one that is free of spelling mistakes and grammatical errors.

▶ *Establish your online presence and be ready to promote it within your Etsy® shop.* Be prepared to share links to other places where you or your business are active on the internet. As you create

tip

The focus of Chapter 5, "Creating Your Product Listings and Product Photography," offers detailed information about how to create product descriptions that sell your products and how to best showcase your products within your shop using the highest-quality images possible.

▶ Introduce Yourself to Your Audience

Placing your profile photo and personal details in the "About" section can be a powerful selling tool for your business. Use a profile photo that clearly showcases your face and depicts you smiling and appearing friendly. The photo could also depict you at work creating whatever it is you will be selling. Consider having a professional portrait taken. Don't simply use a selfie you've taken on your smartphone. After all, it's this photo that will help you establish a positive first impression with your potential customers.

Again, the information within your profile is one way you can humanize your business and share your personal story with potential buyers. As you tell your own story, be sure to:

- ▶ Introduce yourself to your audience and welcome them to your shop.
- ▶ Explain what inspires your work.
- ▶ Describe how you got started.
- ▶ Tell the reader what experience, training, and/or credentials you possess.
- ▶ Explain why you believe your product offerings are special.
- ▶ Invite people to read your blog or company newsletter, visit your personal website, and/ or view online photo albums that showcase your work.
- ▶ Allow visitors to learn more about who you are as a person and where you come from (geographically, as well as philosophically). For example, if you are passionate about creating your products using only eco-friendly materials, don't just state this. Explain how you developed this philosophy, why this approach is important to you personally, and how it impacts your work from a creative or artistic standpoint.

Of course, whatever information you opt to share should somehow be relevant to your work (or your approach to your work), as well as to your company and products. Remember, you're not filling out a profile for an online dating site or trying to make friends with people who enjoy the same books or movies as you.

By conveying a compelling personal story that your target audience will easily relate to, you're more apt to draw in your audience so they'll be more inclined to purchase your items. Obviously, you want to avoid including anything that someone might find offensive or that might create an emotional rift between you and them. So avoid topics relating to religion or politics, for example, unless this information is directly relevant to what you're selling.

your shop, you'll be prompted to provide links and website addresses for your various social media accounts, blog, and/or website. This information all gets displayed under the "Around the Web" heading.

▶ *Define your shop policies.* Start drafting the text that will be displayed below your shop's "Shop Policies" heading. This includes the types of payment you will accept, your shipping options and policies, your refund and exchange policies, as well as access to a company or product-related FAQ (Frequently Asked Questions) document that you, as the seller, can also compose and publish in conjunction with your shop. Be very clear about your various policies and eliminate any concerns a potential customer might have about buying your products.

aha!

When asked to provide keywords and tags, don't just type whatever comes to mind at that moment. Think carefully about the words you select based on what words you believe your target audience will type into a search field when looking for items similar to what you'll be selling.

▶ *Think about search engine optimization (SEO) now.* Provide Etsy® with a list of carefully selected words that perfectly and accurately describe your product(s) and what your company offers. The tags and wording you select are vitally important because they are displayed immediately below the name of your Etsy® shop and help drive traffic to your site.

▶ *Promote yourself.* Be prepared to showcase yourself as the Shop Owner (the artist, artisan, crafter, or curator who is responsible for the items being sold within the shop). In addition to telling your company's story, use this as an opportunity to share your own personal story, philosophy, and values. At the same time, allow people visiting your shop to see what you look like by showcasing a really good photo of yourself within your shop.

Until you have everything prepared properly and ready to publish, do not put your shop online. If you're not totally satisfied with what will be the text elements displayed within your shop, go back and do some reworking or editing.

The process of creating and building an Etsy® shop is explained in the next section. This process involves answering a bunch of questions, providing specific types of information when asked, and importing photos and related content when prompted. As you move forward with this process, be sure to provide what information is requested in each of the appropriate fields.

▶ Fine-Tune and Proofread Your Work

Invest the time needed to create multiple drafts, fine-tune your writing, experiment with different approaches, edit your work, and come up with phrasing that will appeal to your target audience. Then ask a handful of friends or family members who fit into your target audience's demographic to review and critique your work.

Next, seriously consider hiring a professional proofreader or editor to review all the text that will appear within your shop. Explain to the editor or proofreader what you're trying to accomplish and who your target audience is, and then allow them to fine-tune your work and correct all spelling and punctuation errors, plus make recommendations about your word choices, phrasing, and/or writing style.

Based on the initial success of your shop (or lack thereof) and what you learn by interacting with your potential and paying customers, you will likely discover the need to fine-tune, rewrite, or completely overhaul large portions of your text to properly convey your message and accurately describe your products.

Even the most skilled writers typically create multiple drafts of their work prior to publishing it, and then the final draft of that work is carefully reviewed by multiple editors and proofreaders. Because so much importance is placed on the various text elements that will appear within your Etsy® shop, and it's this text that will play a major role in converting traffic to your shop into paying customers, you want the text to be perfect. What you say is as important as how you say it.

The words you use, the writing style you adopt, and the approach you take should be consistent with your brand, be easy to understand, appeal to your target audience, and convey all the vital information that a potential buyer will want or need without needing to spend too much time studying your text and trying to interpret what you meant when writing it. Do not rush the writing, editing, and proofreading process.

Start Building Your Brand by Creating a Logo

The purpose of a logo is to build instant visual brand/company recognition among your potential and paying customers. When displayed within your Etsy® shop, the logo can also be used to showcase your company name in a visual and attention-getting way. Thus, you want to put a lot of thought into the design and appearance of your logo.

Displayed prominently at the top of every Etsy® shop is the shop name, with all spaces taken out. So, the best way to showcase your company name and start establishing your brand on the main page of your Etsy® shop is to also display your company logo (as well as some carefully selected, professional-quality product photos).

While some company logos are simply graphic designs that do not display the company's name (such as the AT&T or Apple logo), based on the way your logo will be displayed within your Etsy® shop, consider somehow including your company name as part of the graphic logo. Simply by browsing through a handful of established Etsy® shops, you will see examples of many different logos and how they've been used to help establish a brand or unique identity for the shop.

Your logo can include your company name displayed in one or more visually interesting and attention-getting fonts. Plus it can (and probably should) include some type of graphic element. Based on your own preference and, more importantly, what you think your target audience will like, your logo can be displayed in full color, in a single solid color, or in black and white.

If you have little or no artistic skill and can't create a professional-looking logo that you believe is capable of representing your company, consider hiring a professional graphic artist. Typically for a predetermined flat fee, you can describe your company and target audience to a graphic artist and then have that person create a handful of logo design options for you. Based on these options, you can have them tweak any of the choices and, once it's perfect, they can provide you with a digital file that will allow you to upload the final logo directly into your Etsy® shop.

Using a freelance service such as Upwork (www.upwork.com), Freelancer.com (www.freelancer.com), DesignCrowd (www.designcrowd.com), Fiverr (www.fiverr.com), or 99Designs (www.99designs.com/projects), you can typically preview portfolios from many graphic artists, find the one you'd like to work with, and then hire them for a fixed price to create your logo.

> **tip**
>
> When hiring a graphic artist to design your logo, make sure the price you agree to includes receiving a handful of initial design options and the ability to have one of the logo options further tweaked. Pay a flat fee for this. Do not pay a graphic artist by the hour.
>
> You then want to receive the finished logo in digital form, saved in one or more common graphic file formats (.jpg, .tif, or .png). You also want it stated, in writing, that the work is 100 percent original and that in exchange for payment, you acquire all legal rights to the logo so you can file for trademark and copyright ownership, if you so choose (which is recommended).

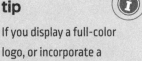

tip

If you display a full-color logo, or incorporate a single color into your logo, this will impact the color scheme and the visual aesthetic of the entire shop. Once you choose a color scheme or visual aesthetic, stick with it throughout your shop and use it to help you establish and promote your overall brand.

If you have trouble finding an affordable graphic designer using one of the online services for finding and hiring freelancers, another approach is to contact a local college with a graphic design program and see if you can hire a student who is looking to build or expand their portfolio.

Other options are to contact and hire a local graphic design firm or use specialized software on your computer that's designed to help nonartistic people design a company logo. To find, purchase, and download this type of software, within any internet search engine, use the search phrase, "logo design software."

Remember, when someone first visits your Etsy® shop, views one of your product listings, or views your Shop Owner Profile, it's probably your logo (as well as your product photography) that will attract their attention first. Make sure the logo allows you to establish a professional and positive first impression.

Establish an Etsy® Seller Account and Initially Create Your Shop

While going through the steps to establish a shop on Etsy® may seem like an extremely important part of the process for launching your business, in reality, this process is no more or less important than the other steps that have been discussed thus far.

The preliminary steps, most of which should be completed before launching your business, include:

▶ Choose the best product(s) to sell that fit nicely on Etsy®.

▶ Find suppliers, distributors, manufacturers, or wholesalers to obtain the tools, supplies, and materials you will need to make whatever it is you'll be selling.

tip

To have an original, professional-looking logo created for your Etsy® shop (and your business), you should not need to spend more than $100. When deciding on a logo, be sure to put yourself into your target audience's shoes and make decisions based on what will appeal to your target audience, even if this goes against what you like personally. If necessary, seek out advice and feedback from people who fit in your target audience (whom you also trust with providing you with their honest opinion) when choosing a final logo design.

▶ Establish yourself as a legal business entity with the government and then obtain a tax identification number.

▶ Identify your target audience.

▶ Determine some of the ways you'll market and advertise your product(s) and shop to your target audience to drive traffic to the shop and generate sales.

▶ Explore other Etsy® shops to see what's possible from a design and functionality standpoint.

▶ Draft the attention-getting, textual content that will appear within your shop.

▶ Take professional-quality photos to showcase your products in your shop.

▶ Consider Using the Official Etsy® Mobile Apps

You'll typically find it easier to handle the majority of the steps for creating and populating your Etsy® shop if you perform them from your internet-enabled desktop or laptop computer using your favorite web browser. However, Etsy® also offers proprietary mobile apps for the iPhone, iPad, and all Android mobile devices that allow you to handle a growing number of these tasks remotely.

The features, functions, and capabilities built into the official Etsy® mobile apps are continuously expanding, so if you have access to a smartphone or tablet, you'll likely discover that many of the tasks involved with creating and managing your Etsy® shop can be done from your mobile device as long as it's connected to the internet.

To download and install the free Etsy® mobile app on your iPhone or iPad, launch the App Store and type "Etsy®" within the Search field. Start by downloading the official Etsy® app. You'll also discover a second official app, called "Sell on Etsy®: Manage Your Shop" that's specifically designed to help sellers manage their Etsy® shops. Be sure to download and install this additional free app as well.

One awesome feature of the Sell on Etsy® app is that you can attach the optional Etsy® Reader to your smartphone or tablet to process in-person credit/debit card sales through Etsy® and keep all your in-person sales information (at craft fairs, for example) linked with your Etsy® sales. To learn more about the free Etsy® Reader, visit: www.Etsy.com/reader.

If you're an Android mobile device user, launch the Google Play Store, tap the App menu, and enter Etsy® in the search field.

In addition to the official Etsy® apps, Etsy® endorses a handful of optional third-party apps that can be useful for creating, managing, and operating your Etsy® shop. To learn more about these apps, which are available from the iOS App Store (iPhone/iPad) and/or Google Play App Store (Android), visit: www.Etsy.com/apps.

▶ Create a logo for your business.

Getting Familiar with Etsy®'s Website

Once you've completed the prerequisite tasks just discussed and before you set up your Etsy® shop, it's a good idea to get familiar with Etsy®'s website. To do so, launch your favorite web browser and visit www.Etsy.com (Figure 4–1, page 67).

The first screen you'll see displays the heading, "Millions of shoppers can't wait to see what you have in store" (Figure 4–2, page 67). This screen provides basic information about what it means to be a seller on Etsy®. It outlines some key benefits, such as the low seller fees, powerful tools, and the free support and educational tools that the Etsy® platform offers to sellers. Simply scroll down the page to review them.

Understand Etsy®'s Fees

Among your costs of doing business are the fees that you, as a seller, will need to pay Etsy®. Unlike other services that allow people to sell items online within their own online shop, Etsy® has no monthly fees and no monthly minimums. As an Etsy® seller, there is a listing fee of $0.20 for every product you opt to showcase within your shop. The next chapter focuses on how to create product listings.

Each listing within your shop stays active for up to four months or until your inventory of that item sells out. So, if you list and showcase one-of-a-kind items within your shop, each time one of those items sells, the listing is closed. However, if you maintain an inventory that includes a large quantity of a particular item, the listing for that item will need to be renewed repeatedly for it to remain active.

Once a customer purchases an item from your shop, as a seller, you pay Etsy® a 3.5 percent transaction fee (based on the selling price) as well as a 3 percent payment-processing fee and an additional $0.25 payment-processing fee.

As you populate your shop with items, the listing fee ($0.20 per item) gets paid upfront. The remaining 6 percent (transaction and payment processing commission combined) and the $0.25 payment processing fee are charged once a sale is made. Be sure to calculate these costs of doing business into your budget, especially when setting your pricing. All Etsy® fees are subject to change. Fees listed here were accurate as of mid-2017.

Setting Up Your Etsy® Account: Required Information

Now it's time to register. Whether you're a buyer or seller on Etsy®, you'll need to create a free account to fully access the service. To do so, go to the Etsy® homepage, click the Register

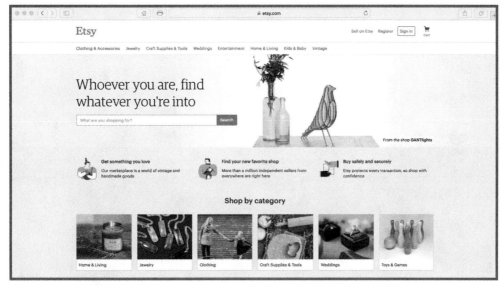

FIGURE 4–1: **Etsy®'s Main Homepage**

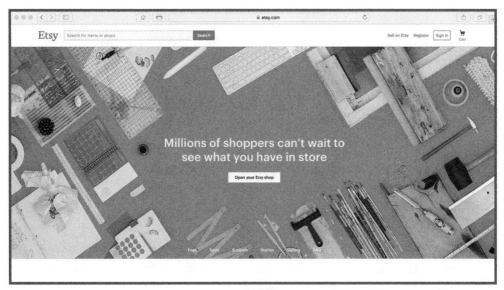

FIGURE 4–2: **Useful Information about Becoming a Seller on Etsy®**

option near the top-right corner, and the "Register/Sign In" pop-up will appear (shown in Figure 4–3, page 68). You can also click the "Open Your Etsy® Shop" button to trigger that same pop-up. Be sure to click the "Register" tab.

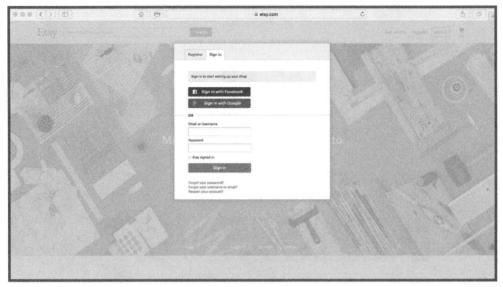

FIGURE 4–3: **Creating Your Free Etsy® Account**
Provide the information that's requested from this Register pop-up window.

You then have the option to create your account using your Facebook or Google account information or to create one from scratch.

To create an Etsy® account from scratch, fill in the information request fields that are displayed within the Register pop-up window:

- ▶ *First Name.* Type your first name.
- ▶ *Last Name.* Type your last name.
- ▶ *Gender.* Options include: Female, Male, or Rather Not Say
- ▶ *Email Address.* Provide your email address.
- ▶ *Password.* Create a password for your account.
- ▶ *Confirm Password.* Re-enter the password to confirm it.
- ▶ *Username.* Create a unique username for your account. This username must not be already in use by any other Etsy® user. If you select a username that's been taken, you'll be prompted to select a different username.

If you want to subscribe to Etsy®'s digital newsletter, add a checkmark to the checkbox that corresponds with the option that says "I want to receive Etsy® Finds, an email newsletter of fresh trends and editors' picks."

Click the Register button to activate your Etsy® account. An email will be sent to the account you provided. Upon receipt, click the "Confirm Account" button to confirm your email address.

After signing into your Etsy® account and clicking the "Sell on Etsy®" bar, the Etsy® service will walk you through the shop creation process, which consists of the following five main steps:

1. Shop preferences
2. Name your shop
3. Stock your shop
4. How you'll get paid
5. Set up billing

Take your time with each of these steps and be sure to provide accurate and complete information. If your shop's content is complete per the instructions just provided (i.e., text, photos, logo, etc.), you'll be able to complete each step rather quickly.

Step 1: Set Your Shop Preferences Options

From the Shop Preferences web browser screen (shown in Figure 4–4), select your primary language, country, and shop currency from displayed pull-down menus. Click on each option, one at a time, and make your selection.

For example, if you speak English and live in the United States, your selections should be, English, United States, and United States Dollar, respectively.

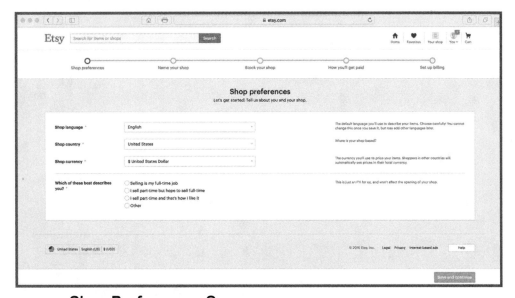

FIGURE 4–4: **Shop Preferences Screen**
Choose your desired options.

For the question that asks, "Which of these best describes you?" select one of the displayed options. Click on the Save and Continue button that's displayed near the very bottom-right corner of the page to proceed.

Step 2: *Provide the Name of Your Shop*

Here, it's essential that you select a unique company/shop name that's attention getting, that describes what your shop offers, and/or that somehow reflects your style as a seller (shown in Figure 4–5).

When it comes to creating a shop/company name, it can describe the product you're selling, such as JasonRichPhotography or JewelryByJoanne, or it can also be a more abstract name (that incorporates an originally coined word or phrase). This second approach, however, doesn't allow a new visitor to quickly understand what your shop offers.

Think carefully about your shop name. Make sure it will appeal to your target audience and is memorable as well as easy to spell. Because your shop name will be displayed

tip

Your company logo, which is a graphic file that you upload to be displayed in your shop, will ultimately be positioned alongside the displayed shop name, and the logo can showcase your shop name any way you see fit and include the use of graphics or color, for example.

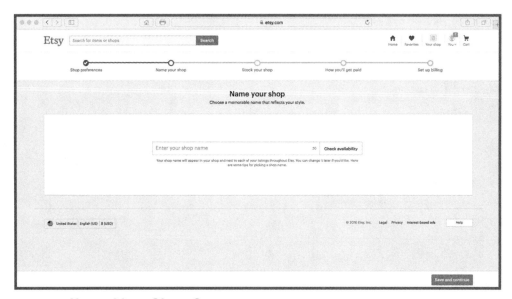

FIGURE 4–5: **Name Your Shop Screen**

Type your desired shop name. Do not include spaces.

with no spaces, use upper and lowercase letters to make it easier to read. For example, the shop name, "Jason Rich Photography," will be displayed as "JasonRichPhotography." This is much easier to read than, "jasonrichphotography" or "JASONRICHPHOTOGRAPHY."

Within the field provided, type your desired shop name. If a green and white graphic appears to the right of the field that says, "Available," you're free to proceed. Otherwise, you will be prompted to enter an alternate name. Click on the Save and Continue button that's displayed in the lower-right corner of the screen to continue.

Step 3: Stock Your Shop

In this step, you create individual listings for each product you plan to sell in your Etsy® shop. To begin creating one listing at a time, click the "+ Add a Listing" option (shown

▶ Consider Your Shop Name Carefully

A shop name must be between four and 20 characters long, with no spaces, and should offer a combination of upper and lowercase letters. The shop name you select must also be unique. It cannot be the same as any other shop that already exists on Etsy®, and your shop name should not violate anyone else's trademarks or copyrights. It's also a good strategy to avoid using a shop name that's extremely similar to another shop on Etsy®, or you could wind up confusing the buyers.

Even if the shop name is available for use on Etsy®, use an internet search engine, such as Google or Yahoo!, and enter the name you want to use. Make sure it's not being used by a company operating outside of the Etsy® platform.

Next, visit the website for the United States Patent and Trademark Office (www.uspto.gov/trademark) and search the trademark database (www.uspto.gov/trademarks-application-process/search-trademark-database) to make sure no other business already owns the name you want to use.

Ultimately, you may want to register your company name as a copyright and/or trademark to protect your legal rights to that name in the future. You can file the appropriate forms entirely by yourself, hire a copyright or trademark attorney to handle this task for you, or use a fee-based online service, such as LegalZoom (www.legalzoom.com), as a less expensive alternative to a lawyer, to help you with the filing process.

For additional tips from Etsy® on how to choose a shop name, visit: www.Etsy.com/seller-handbook/article/top-tips-for-choosing-your-Etsy-shop/23181234159.

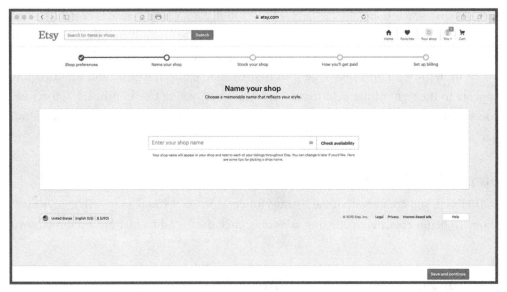

FIGURE 4–6: **Show Preferences Screen**

in Figure 4–6). Keep in mind, a charge of $0.20 applies to each listing you create and publish.

One at a time, create product listings for each product you plan to showcase and sell within your shop.

The process of creating detailed, accurate, and attention-getting product listings and showcasing professional-quality product photos with each listing is an extremely important one. Thus, the entire focus of Chapter 5, "Creating Your Product Listings and Product Photography," covers this step. Once a product listing has been created and published online, you always have the option of editing it or removing it from your shop.

Step 4: How You'll Get Paid

The goal of any Etsy® shop is to sell your items and generate revenue. When a buyer makes a purchase from your shop, the funds are collected by Etsy® and then forwarded to you (the seller). This step involves providing the banking information needed so Etsy® can send you the money you earn.

First, you'll be prompted to select which payment options you want to accept from your buyers. Options include credit/debit cards, PayPal, Etsy® Gift Cards, and Apple Pay, if you're located within the United States. Based on which options you choose, additional transaction fees may apply. You can also opt to have buyers mail you a check or money

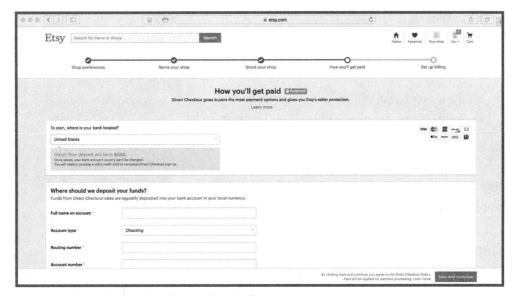

FIGURE 4–7: **The How You'll Get Paid Screen**
Share information about your bank account with Etsy® when prompted.

order directly. As a new seller, take advantage of all the payment options Etsy® allows you to offer to your buyers.

From the "How You'll Get Paid" screen, click on the pull-down menu and select the appropriate option related to the question, "Where is your bank located?" Based on your response, additional fields will now be displayed (see Figure 4–7).

Be sure to provide complete and accurate information within each field. You'll be prompted to enter the Full Name on Account (which is the name that the personal or business bank account is registered to). Next, select the Account Type. Your options include: Checking or Savings.

By looking in the lower-left corner of a blank check from your checking account, viewing your bank statement, or contacting your bank, you can easily determine your bank's routing number and the number of the account to which you want your Etsy® sales deposited. Remember, if you want to collect your money from Etsy® as you make sales, this requested information must be entered accurately.

Next, scroll down to the "Tell Us a Little Bit About Yourself" heading, and then fill in all the following fields:

▶ Country of residence
▶ First name

- ► Last name
- ► Date of birth (month, day, and year)
- ► The last four digits of your Social Security number
- ► Your home address
- ► Your phone number (which can be your cell number, home number, or work number)

Then click the Save and Continue button that is displayed in the bottom-right corner of the screen to proceed.

tip

If the information you provide cannot be electronically verified by Etsy®, you will be prompted to scan and upload a copy of your government-issued identification.

Step 5: Set Up Billing

This final step requires you to provide your own credit/debit card information (or PayPal account information), which will be used to pay your ongoing Etsy® charges, such as your listing fees.

Once you complete all five of the steps outlined in this chapter, you're ready to open your shop for business. Simply click on the Open Your Shop button that appears in the lower-right corner of the screen to do this.

Your Etsy® Shop Has a Unique Website Address

Once the initial shop setup is complete, there is one more mandatory feature to add: a unique website address. When you click the Open Your Shop button, you'll see Etsy® provides your shop with a unique website address (URL) in one of these two formats:

www.Etsy.com/shop/yourshopname
https://yourshopname.Etsy.com

This is the website URL you can begin promoting and giving out to potential buyers. However, you also have the option of registering your own easier-to-remember domain name using any domain name registrar and then forwarding that new domain name to your Etsy® shop URL.

warning

Do not open your shop to the public until you have proofread everything. Use the shop preview tools to see exactly what your shop will look like before it's open and accessible to the public. Once your shop is open, however, you always have the option of updating or editing any of the content within it.

▶ Register and Forward Your Own Website URL

Instead of promoting your Etsy® shop domain name as www.Etsy.com/shop/yourshopname or https://yourshopname.Etsy.com, you can visit the website of any domain name registrar, such as GoDaddy.com, and register your own easier-to-remember domain name.

For example, if your Etsy®-assigned shop URL is www.Etsy.com/shop/jasonrichphotography, and you want to register the domain name www.jasonrichphotography.com or www.jasonrich. photography, for example, this can be done separately for an additional annual fee. You can then forward the domain name(s) you acquire to your Etsy® shop URL using the domain registrar's forwarding tools.

To do this, visit a domain name registrar, such as www.godaddy.com, and determine if the domain name you want is available. If so, you will have the opportunity to register the domain name (for an annual fee) and then forward the newly acquired domain name to your Etsy® shop's assigned URL. By doing this, you can obtain a domain name that is simply a word or phrase, followed by the domain extension you select, such as .com, .shop, .info, or .photography.

While literally hundreds of domain extensions are available, most web surfers (especially non-tech-savvy ones) automatically stick a .com at the end of the website they want to visit. For this reason, it's in your best interest to use a website URL that ends with .com. However, you can also register the same domain name with multiple extensions (for an additional annual fee).

Adding Additional Information

The initial five steps you just completed are all mandatory. However, you now have the ability to add extra content to your shop. This optional content is very important because it allows you to share more information about you and your company and better address the wants, needs, and concerns of your visitors.

Add Your Shop's "About" Section

To begin populating your shop's "About" section, you must first open your shop to the public. Then, after signing into your Etsy® account, click the Your Shop

aha!

Make sure every story includes a one-sentence headline to grab the reader's attention and make a statement that will encourage them to keep reading.

button that's located in the top-right corner of the screen. Then click the Edit Shop option, scroll down, and click on the "About" section.

Populate the "About" section with your company's information. Tell your story by adding text to the "Shop Story" section. Be sure to tell your story in an upbeat and interesting way and use this as a tool to humanize your business to begin building a virtual community around your shop and the products you're offering. Talk about why you created your shop, how you selected the products you're selling, what's unique about your products (or the approach you take to making them), and provide any interesting anecdotes you think your target audience would like to know.

The "Story" section can be up to 5,000 characters long. However, you're not only limited to text. Etsy® offers the ability to upload and display photos or a video to the "Story" section to help you tell yours.

You can use photos or videos in the "About" section to explain how your products are made or demonstrate how they can be used. As with your product photos, any photos or videos you share should be high quality so they don't take away from your credibility as a business operator.

Set Your Shop Policies

As you read earlier, the "Shop Policies" section is where you can answer common questions from buyers by providing answers before they're asked. For example, your shop policies should include details about your return policy, exchange policy, product warranty, and product guarantee. It's here you should also describe the shipping options you offer to buyers, the processing time orders will be filled and shipped, the payment options you accept, and your shop's privacy policy (if applicable).

To add Shop Policies to your Etsy® shop, click the Your Shop button that's displayed at the top of the screen, select the Edit Shop option, and then choose the Shop Policies option.

Explain Your Shipping Options and Policies

Once a buyer decides to make a purchase from your shop, one of their primary concerns will relate to shipping. Following are some potential buyer questions:

- ▶ How quickly will their order ship?
- ▶ What shipping method will be used?
- ▶ How much do you charge for shipping and handling?
- ▶ What insurance do you include with a shipped package?
- ▶ How can a shipment be tracked?

tip

To learn more about Etsy® shipping profiles and how to create them, visit: www. Etsy.com/help/article/190.

The shipping-related information you provide is displayed in conjunction with your shop policies. However, some shipping information also gets displayed as part of each product listing.

When providing shipping information, it's important to be upfront and honest with your buyers. For example, only state that you fill and ship orders on the same day they're placed if this is true, you have the product(s) in stock, and you're able to process each order and get it shipped that same day.

If you make items to order or offer custom orders, make it clear to your buyers what the manufacturing time will be and when they can expect their order to be shipped. This is referred to as the order "processing time."

To make it easier to add information about shipping rates and options, Etsy® allows sellers to create shipping profiles. This allows the Etsy® service to automatically calculate a customer's shipping charges based on information you provide and the details of the customer's specific order.

Link Your Social Media Account to Your Shop

Chapter 6, "Promoting and Marketing Your Etsy® Shop," focuses on the ways you can utilize paid advertising as well as social media (Facebook, Twitter, Instagram, Pinterest, etc.) to drive traffic to your shop.

In addition to using social media as a way to drive new traffic to your site, you can also use these services to stay in touch with your existing customers and potentially generate

aha!

As social media services evolve, the process for linking your Etsy® shop to your account on each service will change. For the most up-to-date directions for linking your Etsy® shop with your social media accounts, visit: www.Etsy.com/help/article/1439.

repeat business. Thus, in your Etsy® shop, you'll definitely want to display links to your social media accounts, as well as other marketing venues you may have such as your company website, company or personal blog, company newsletter, and/or your company's YouTube channel.

To display these links within your Etsy® shop, log into your Etsy® account, click on the Your Shop button, select the Shop Settings option, click the Info and Appearances option, and then click the Links option. One at a time, add each website, blog, or social media account URL that you want to display in your shop.

Keep in mind, each Facebook page or Twitter account can only be linked with one Etsy® shop, and the first time you attempt to establish the link you will be asked to grant permission to Etsy® to link with each account.

Add Sections to Your Shop

If you will be selling more than one item within your shop or selling items that fit into different product categories, it's possible to divide up and categorize each of your product listings into sections. For example, if you're a jewelry maker, you might include individual sections for bracelets, necklaces, earrings, rings, and charms.

More information about organizing and showcasing your products is offered in Chapter 5. You can also learn more about how to create, edit, and delete sections within your shop by visiting: www.Etsy.com/help/article/165.

Just as a bookshop has different sections for fiction, nonfiction, biographies, reference books, graphic novels,

tip

Adding sections to your Etsy® shop is particularly important if you have more than a dozen products and not all of your products fit into the same category. The more products you have, the more specialized sections you'll want to create so your shop looks less cluttered visually and buyers will have an easier time finding exactly what they're shopping for.

For example, if you're a jewelry maker and a buyer is looking for a bracelet, they should not have to browse through several dozen listings for necklaces or rings to see your bracelet offerings. They should be able to click the "Bracelets" Section, and see just your selection of bracelets.

children's books, etc., your Etsy® shop can have different sections, which makes it easier for a buyer to browse your shop for the specific items or types of products they're looking for.

Add Shop Updates on a Regular Basis

Etsy® encourages sellers to regularly update their shops using the Shop Updates feature, introduced in late 2015. It is included in the official Sell on Etsy® mobile app. In a nutshell, it allows you to snap a new photo of your product and then quickly link it with a product listing in your shop. That newly added photo can then easily be published and shared simultaneously on all your social media accounts without ever leaving the Sell on Etsy® app.

Use Shop Updates to take lifestyle photos of your products, for example, and quickly add them to your shop and social media accounts. Update photos are in addition to the five product photos that can be featured with each product listing.

All Shop Updates get automatically displayed within your shop's homepage, under the "Shop Updates" section, which appears below the "About" section, and are displayed in the order they're published. To learn more about this feature and discover ways to utilize it to better showcase and promote your individual products, visit: www.Etsy.com/seller-handbook/article/5-tips-for-sharing-your-story-with-shop/31380092335.

Create Your Personal Profile

As a shop owner, artist, creator, maker, or artisan, your customers will want to know about you personally. They'll want to know your back story, what inspires your work, what skills and education you have, what your philosophies related to your work are, and other information that will help them better appreciate and value whatever it is you're selling.

In addition to your company's story, Etsy® allows every user to create a personal profile to share information. As a seller, this is another tool you can use to win over your potential customers, differentiate yourself from your competition, and showcase yourself as an expert in your field, for example.

To create, add to, or edit your personal profile, which includes the ability to showcase your photo, log into your Etsy® account and then click the You button that's displayed near the top-right corner of the screen. Next, click the Account Settings option and then click the Public Profile option (that's displayed on the left side of the screen).

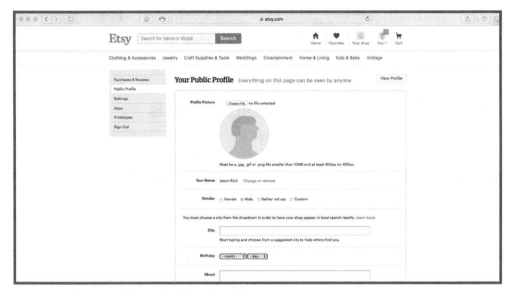

FIGURE 4–8: **Create Your Public Profile**

Every Etsy® seller should create and populate their Profile page with relevant information about themselves.

From the "Your Public Profile" page (shown in Figure 4–8), you're prompted to upload a profile photo. This should be a headshot that clearly shows your face and that's been saved in the .jpg, .gif, or .png file format. The digital image's file size can be up to 10MB, and the resolution should be at least 400 by 400 pixels.

Next, you have the option to determine exactly how your full name will be displayed. Based on your personal preference, you might opt to display only your first name. However, many buyers will appreciate knowing the full name of the person they're buying from, so seriously consider displaying your full name.

If you have not already done so when setting up your Etsy® account, include your gender. From the "Your Public Profile" screen, you can choose between Female, Male, Rather Not Say, or Custom. If you select "Custom," fill in the field that applies to the gender you want to be identified as.

Next, choose your city. Begin typing the city where your business is located (or where you live), and select the most accurate option that gets displayed. Keep in mind, the majority of the information you provide within your profile is not only displayed when someone opts to view your profile, but each piece of information also becomes searchable.

You will be prompted to enter your birthday (month and day only). You can also type text that describes you and share your personal story in the "About" field. Then, within the Favorite Materials field, you're able to list up to 13 materials (each separated by a comma) that you like to work with as an artist, crafter, maker, manufacturer, or artisan.

Finally, you can choose where Etsy® users will be able to view your profile from. Because you're trying to drive as much traffic to your shop as possible and obtain as much attention as you can get, your best strategy is to check each of the boxes provided.

Before saving your changes, click the View Profile button to preview what your profile will look like. Once again, proofread absolutely everything before publishing it online. If satisfied, click the Save Changes button and your newly updated profile will be published online and immediately become viewable by Etsy® users.

Remember to Focus on Your Target Audience

Throughout this book you have been encouraged to provide all of the information that Etsy® requests and to be as accurate and detailed as possible. This is definitely a viable strategy for helping you generate the most attention possible from people using the Etsy® service, including your potential customers.

You also need to understand that web surfers and online shoppers in general have no patience and a very short attention span. You want to convey the most relevant information possible using the fewest words so people can get the information they need and quickly find exactly what they're looking for.

If you can concisely explain something in one sentence, don't use a paragraph or more of text in your shop to convey specific information. Understand who your target audience is, provide the information you believe is most relevant and useful, and be respectful of your audience's time. If information isn't directly relevant, avoid sharing it.

For example, don't share information about your favorite books, movies, or TV shows in your company or personal profile unless this information is directly relevant to what you're selling and it pertains to your story in a way that your audience will find informative, enlightening, or entertaining.

warning

Ultimately, every word, sentence, headline, description, photo, graphic, color scheme, aesthetic element, or other piece of content that gets displayed in your shop should cater directly to your target audience. If you're not properly using Etsy®'s various features, functions, and tools to cater to your target audience, even if you're offering superior products, you will lose sales and could potentially alienate a visitor to your shop.

Meet Joanne Simmons, Proprietor of SilverSculptor

Joanne Simmons is a talented jewelry maker who has an established online business selling her creations via Etsy® (www.Etsy.com/shop/SilverSculptor). One of the unique aspects of Simmons's work is that she creates one-of-a-kind jewelry pieces using the imprint of a child's hand. However, she also offers original jewelry pieces, including necklaces, bracelets, earrings, rings, and cufflinks, all handcrafted from silver, as you can see in Figure 4–9.

"I am originally from London, England, and I moved to the United States in 2005, says Simmons. "I had a corporate job, but it was not allowing me to utilize my creativity or pursue my artistic passions. I wanted to pursue a hobby that would prevent me from just sitting in front of the television during my free time who now resides in Jersey City, New Jersey.

"On one Saturday afternoon, I was exploring the Etsy® service, and I discovered some jewelry that I really liked. I learned about the materials used to make the jewelry I liked, and then I took some jewelry-making classes to learn how to make similar items myself. Over time, I wound up making jewelry for myself and my friends. I personally like silver jewelry but could not find jewelry designs in traditional shops that matched my taste. Having pursued jewelry making as a hobby, I wound up stockpiling my creations and had nothing to do with them."

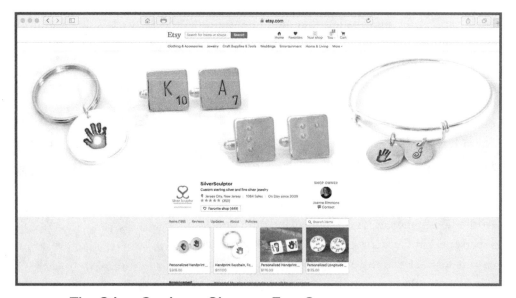

FIGURE 4–9: **The SilverSculptor Shop on Etsy®**

After learning about a craft fair in her community, Simmons decided to set up a booth and showcase her silver jewelry designs for the first time. "I was astonished by how many people really liked my designs and bought my jewelry at that craft fair. That's when I decided to establish a presence on Etsy® and start selling my jewelry online. This was back in 2010," she says.

Several years after establishing her Etsy® business and operating it as a hobby on a part-time basis, Simmons was downsized from her corporate job and decided to pursue jewelry making and selling her products online as a full-time job. "With the extra time on my hands, I was able to create new products, plus invest the time needed to properly market my online business and create proper listings for each product within my Etsy® shop," says Simmons.

In addition to maintaining her presence on Etsy®, Simmons continues to participate in at least two major craft fairs per year, as well as several smaller craft fairs. She's also developed a relationship with several jewelry shops that are currently selling her jewelry. "Whenever I am selling my jewelry in person at craft fairs, I always distribute business cards that list the website address for my Etsy® shop. However, I typically sell different jewelry designs online versus what I sell at the craft fairs in person. I have found that the craft fairs attract different clientele than the people who shop on Etsy®," she says.

"On Etsy®, my clients tend to be women who are engaged and soon to be married, as well as women who have recently given birth to a child. My experience is that people shop on Etsy® because they're looking for items that are unique and that are personalized. People who shop on Etsy® know that they can contact the shop owner and receive a personal response to a question or request. This is a different experience than what someone has when shopping for jewelry at a retail shop or at a crafts fair, for example," explains Simmons.

Over the years, Simmons' product line has evolved. New jewelry designs or product categories often come about based on suggestions or requests from her customers. For example, one of her more popular product types are handcrafted men's cufflinks with personalized designs. "The idea for cufflinks came about as a result of a special request from a client a few years ago. I created personalized cufflinks for that client but discovered a demand for this type of product. My female clients buy cufflinks as a gift for a special man in their life," she states.

"I definitely recommend paying attention to the requests, questions, and feedback you receive as a seller on Etsy® because your interaction with potential or existing customers can often lead to ideas for new products or ways to improve on existing products," says Simmons. "I encourage people on Etsy® to contact me with special product requests or customizations."

Back when Simmons opened her Etsy® shop, she recalls that Etsy® was less commercial. The service focused mainly on artisans selling handcrafted goods. Simmons explains, "Back then, I found Etsy® provided more of an online community where sellers often supported each other. Since then, the service has expanded its focus. Because I started my online shop via Etsy® early on, I think it was easier back then to get established and get noticed on the service. I think someone first starting to sell items on Etsy® today faces more challenges."

Back when she started selling her jewelry on Etsy® as a part-time hobby, Simmons had no expectations. She recalled that it took some time to get the first few sales, but after receiving positive feedback from her first customers, orders started to trickle in at a faster and more regular pace.

"People shopping on Etsy® pay attention to a seller's ratings and reviews. Once you have a handful of positive reviews, it boosts your online credibility," says Simmons.

"When you first launch your online shop on Etsy®, I recommend selling a few items to your friends or people you know and ask them to provide positive but honest reviews so you can establish yourself online a bit faster.

"Customers shopping on Etsy® put a lot of weight on reviews when making their purchase decisions. Especially if you have competition online selling similar products, having lots of positive reviews will help boost your credibility. It's important to understand that once a customer receives the product(s) you sold, they only have a small window during which they're allowed to write and publish a review on Etsy®. As a seller, you want to encourage your customers to provide reviews quickly," says Simmons.

"I often receive emails from customers immediately after they receive their order telling me how much they love their purchase. I always use this opportunity to politely ask them to write a review and publish it on Etsy®. Sometimes they do this, but I have found that only a small percentage of my customers will write and publish a review even if they are thrilled with their purchase," she adds. "When I send my customers an email with their order tracking information, I include a reminder for them to write a review. I do not, however, send a follow-up email in conjunction with each order asking for a review unless someone contacts me first. This is my personal preference in terms of the approach. As of late 2016, I have had more than 1,000 sales through Etsy® but have received only about 250 online reviews."

Looking back to when she first launched her Etsy® shop, Simmons recalls it took her almost a month before she received her first order. "If I were to launch my Etsy® shop today, what I would do differently is focus heavily on promoting my business using social media. I didn't start using social media to promote my business until almost two years after I launched it. Social media marketing is definitely something that all Etsy® shop owners need to focus on. My social media presence now includes Pinterest, Facebook, Twitter, and Instagram. For me, Instagram and Pinterest generate the best results in terms of generating new customers, although Facebook and Twitter also continue to be powerful marketing tools," says Simmons.

Instagram and Pinterest offer useful tools for posting and sharing product photos. "I post something new every day on each social media service. I typically publish the same or similar posts on each service because I have different followers on each. However, I know I could probably benefit more if I posted original content on each service," she adds.

While social media serves as a useful and cost-effective marketing tool for Simmons' SilverSculptor business on Etsy®, when it comes to maintaining her online shop, she believes that branding is essential. "You need to showcase a professional-looking logo and design your shopfront so it appeals to your target audience. Everything related to your business should maintain a professional and cohesive appearance. One extremely important component of an Etsy® shopfront is your product photography. It should have a highly professional appearance and showcase your work in vivid detail," explains Simmons.

In terms of branding her Etsy® shopfront, Simmons chose an overall color scheme that incorporates a lot of gray because it goes nicely with the silver color of her jewelry. She adds, "For my product photos, I typically use a white or slate background. I use the same color scheme for my product packaging so it helps define an overall brand image. Once you have a logo created for your business, it should appear everywhere—in your Etsy® shop, on your product packaging, on your letterhead and business cards, and in your social media."

Simmons has always had a passion for photography, so she takes her own product shots as a way to further express her creativity. "I had to learn how to take professional-looking photos of my jewelry because the photography skill and approach for product shots is very different than taking photos of people or landscapes, for example. It is absolutely essential that your product photos look amazing. If you compare my early product photos to the product photos currently appearing in my Etsy® shop, you'll see how I have fine-tuned and enhanced my product photography skills over time. I definitely recommend using a white or minimalist background when taking product shots so you don't take attention away from the product itself," says Simmons.

She adds, "In addition to traditional product shots with a solid white or slate background, I also showcase my products being worn by people so I incorporate lifestyle product photos as well. If you don't have the appropriate digital photography equipment, as well as the photography skill, to take your own professional-quality product shots, I definitely recommend hiring a professional photographer to take your product shots for you so that you're able to achieve the highest quality shots possible. To save money, you can always go to a local community college that offers a photography program and see if you can work with a photography student who is looking to expand their portfolio.

"While you could invest in a high-end digital SLR camera to take product shots, I have found that the rear-facing camera built into one of the newer iPhone models can allow you to create impressive results when taking your own product shots. You don't have to spend a fortune to create high-quality product photos. I created my own light box and often use a piece of white poster board to create my seamless white background. I also use a tripod and the camera timer so I am not touching, moving or shaking the camera at all when I'm actually taking a photo.

"I have also discovered that when taking my own product shots, it's easier to take advantage of natural light as opposed to artificial light from light bulbs. If you do use light bulbs, make sure they generate white light. Also, be sure to adjust the white balance within your digital camera so that your white backgrounds look crisp, clear, and bright white."

As a business owner, Simmons believes that it's important to ultimately develop all the skills needed to run a business. This includes learning how to take your own product shots so you're not reliant on other people in the long term.

"I had to learn how to do all my own bookkeeping, for example. When you first start your own Etsy® business, remember that you are establishing a real-life business. This means you need to set it up as a business from day one and keep all the proper financial records, for example. Set yourself up as a business with a proper bank account and tax ID number from the IRS and local or state government. The more knowledge you have about accounting, bookkeeping, marketing, and general business, the more of an advantage you'll have when you launch your online business whether it's through Etsy® or another service," says Simmons, who hires an accountant at the end of each year to help her properly prepare her business' tax returns for the IRS.

Now that Simmons has an established and successful Etsy® business, she spends about half her time managing the online aspects of her business, taking product shots, doing her social media marketing, and interacting with potential and existing customers. The remainder of her time is spent actually creating jewelry and maintaining or expanding her inventory.

When it comes to pricing her products, Simmons started off by keeping her prices low because she didn't have the confidence in her own work to charge premium prices. Over the years since she started, however, she's built up much more confidence in her work and now feels comfortable charging appropriate prices for her handcrafted work.

"Since this is now my full-time job, I needed to adjust my prices so I could sustain a full-time income from the work I'm doing as well as give myself the ability to sell my products at wholesale prices to retail jewelry shops and still earn a profit. These days, I have worked out my pricing so I earn approximately $20 per hour for my labor. So, to set my pricing, I figure out my total cost to create a piece, including materials and labor, and then I double that to set my wholesale price. Then I double my wholesale price to set my retail price. This is the formula that I have found works for my business."

Until recently, Simmons' main marketing efforts revolved around posting content on social media. Only in the past year has she begun to experiment with paid online advertising through Facebook, for example, as a way to generate traffic to her business's own website, which in turn promotes her shop on Etsy®.

"I created a separate website because I do not want to rely 100 percent on Etsy® for the success or failure of my business. Etsy® has a lot of rules that sellers need to adhere to. By also having my own website, I have more freedom to directly showcase and sell my products. While Etsy® is a strong and stable company, it could theoretically shut down for some reason at any time. If that were to happen, I'd be out of business as well if I didn't also have my own ecommerce website. The standalone website focuses mainly on my custom handprint jewelry, but I am looking to expand what I use it for while continuing to maintain my Etsy® shop," says Simmons.

As an online service, Etsy® has become very popular around the world with both buyers and sellers. This means that for almost any type of product that's being sold, a seller will have competition on Etsy® that sells similar products, as well as competition from products sold elsewhere online and through traditional retail shops.

"I continuously do research to determine what my competition is doing, says Simmons. "For example, I analyze what keywords are used by my competition within their titles, product descriptions, and listings. I try to determine why other sellers sometimes achieve a better position in the search results than my products. However, I don't focus too much on the jewelry designs that my competition offers. I don't want to be influenced in any way by other jewelry designs."

On a day-to-day basis, Simmons really enjoys the contact and interaction she has with her potential and existing customers. It's the positive feedback she receives from her customers that gives her the most satisfaction.

"Knowing that I am somehow creating some joy in someone's life whenever they wear my jewelry is very rewarding to me," adds Simmons, who recommends that new Etsy® sellers take advantage of the free information provided by Etsy® through their Etsy® Success online newsletter and YouTube channel. "These resources offer a lot of very useful information that sellers will find valuable. The Sell on Etsy® app also offers a Shop Update tool that's very useful for updating content on an Etsy® shopfront."

Additional Thoughts

As you establish your Etsy® shop (or any other online presence), be sure to utilize the tools offered to you in the appropriate way. If you're prompted to fill in information fields with specific content, for example, stick to what's requested. Don't try to use any of the tools provided in a way that it was not designed to be used for. Take advantage of the tools provided to help you draw in your audience and ultimately help you sell your product(s). In the next chapter, the focus is on creating your specific product listings and utilizing the best possible product photography.

Creating Your Product Listings and Product Photography

In the previous chapter, you learned the basic steps required to establish your shop on Etsy®, brand that shop using your company logo, and customize the shop by adding various customized content and elements. All of that was in preparation for populating your shop with information about the actual items you plan to sell.

tip

Each item you plan to sell must have its own product listing within your shop, whether you have one of that specific item to sell or an unlimited supply. Items that are similar, but not the same, must each have their own product listing.

When it comes to presenting your shop visitors with information about the specific items you're selling, you use individual product listings. Groups of similar product listings can then be categorized and sorted into sections, so they become easier to find and get presented to your visitors in a clutter-free, easy-to-find way.

An Etsy® shop can contain as many separate product listings as you desire, although you pay a flat fee of $0.20 per product listing. Remember, each product listing remains active in your store until you're sold out of the item, or for four months, whichever comes first.

Each product listing is comprised of several key elements, all of which are equally important because each is used in a slightly different way to attract traffic to your shop and showcase each item to your visitors. These elements include:

- ▶ Product photos
- ▶ Title
- ▶ Information about the listing (who made it, what it is, and when it was made)
- ▶ Product category
- ▶ Price
- ▶ The quantity you have available
- ▶ The type of item it is
- ▶ Product description
- ▶ Section
- ▶ Variations (such as colors or sizes available)
- ▶ Shipping options
- ▶ Search terms

tip

As you create each product listing, you must choose whether you plan to manually renew the listing yourself or you want the listing to automatically renew when it expires (for an additional fee of $0.20). If you have more than one of an item to sell, the listing will renew automatically when one unit is sold until your inventory on hand sells out. You will be charged the $0.20 relisting fee each time.

While you can compose the required text that will ultimately fill in each field of a product listing off the top of your head as you're creating each listing, a much better approach is to invest the time to prewrite all the necessary text, edit it, tweak it, proofread it, and make sure it perfectly caters to your target audience all before you publish it online.

Remember, when you sell anything online, your customers do not have the opportunity to touch, smell, test out, or experience the item firsthand. What they have to rely on is their past experience with similar items, as well as what you (the seller) say about it, what they see in your product photos, and what ratings and reviews you have received from past buyers.

While your visitors want plenty of detailed and accurate information about each product, they also want it presented to them quickly, concisely, and in a manner that's easy to find and understand. If a potential customer needs to invest more than a few seconds searching for a specific product or seeking out an answer to a question that's on their mind, chances are they'll simply leave your shop and seek the item they want elsewhere.

Because a lot of your time, money, and effort will ultimately be spent marketing and advertising your Etsy® shop, it's your responsibility to do absolutely everything possible to convert that traffic into paying customers, or your marketing and advertising efforts will all be for nothing.

To generate a demand for each of your items and convince your potential customer they should want or that they absolutely need what you're selling right away, the following are some of the pertinent questions that you want to answer somewhere in each of your product listings:

- ▶ What is the item you're selling?
- ▶ How does the item work?
- ▶ What size, color, or customizable options are available?
- ▶ What does the item look like, feel like, and/or smell like (if applicable)?
- ▶ How much is it?
- ▶ Why should the potential buyer want your product? How will it help them address a want or need?
- ▶ Does the item make a good gift? If so, for whom? Why is it a great gift?
- ▶ What specifically sets your item apart from others?
- ▶ What are the key benefits of your item?
- ▶ How is the item made, and what is it made of?
- ▶ What are some of the ways the item can best be used?
- ▶ Why should a potential customer purchase your item right away?
- ▶ How does the item come packaged?
- ▶ If someone places their order today, when can they expect to receive it?
- ▶ What's unique or special about the manufacturing process or the materials it's made from?
- ▶ What exactly is included with the item?

Even if a fact about your item seems obvious to you or is clearly displayed within a product photo, you still should explain the basics using language that anyone in your target audience will easily understand.

What You Say and How You Say It Are Equally Important

The language, approach, and writing style you use for your product listings should be carefully crafted for your target audience. At the same time, everything in the product listing should take on an upbeat, sales-oriented approach with descriptive wording.

If your product is handcrafted, for example, consider using words and phrases such as "handcrafted," "handmade," "one-of-a-kind," "unique," "top-quality," "highest quality," "exclusive," "distinctive," "rare," "exceptional craftsmanship," "superior craftsmanship," "made from the finest materials," "made from all-natural materials," and "made in the USA" to describe what you're selling.

Remember, using words, you want to describe what you're selling in detail. Ideally, you want to tap into the reader's five senses (sight, smell, touch, taste, and hearing) and help them relate directly to what you're selling. As appropriate, answer questions such as: How does it look? How much does it weigh? What does it feel like? What does it smell like? How does it taste? What sounds does it make? How will it make someone feel?

One of your goals should be to use descriptive words and phrases, as well as your product photos, to help each visitor relate directly to what you're offering. Try to elicit a fond memory of a familiar and good feeling or directly address a known want or need, while creating an urgency for the buyer to acquire it immediately.

Consider using a thesaurus to help you select powerful and descriptive words that apply to your product and that will help add a sense of urgency and time sensitivity to your potential customers' want or need for it. For example, use phrases such as "limited quantity available," "this one-of-a-kind item is in high demand," "save 20% if you order right now," "guaranteed delivery by [insert holiday], if you order today," or "be among the first to own a piece from this groundbreaking collection."

aha!

As you're writing your product listings, pretend you're speaking directly with your potential customer in person. Anticipate what information they'd want to know, and present it to them in a way that will quickly get them excited about what you're selling.

Using the appropriate words and phrases within your product listings, you also want to convey a sense of quality, assuring your customer that the item is safe and built to last. Use words and phrases such as "guaranteed," "hassle-free," "no-questions-asked returns," "lifetime warranty," "authentic," "tested," "unconditional," "no risk," "no obligation," "money back," "refund," "secure," "safe," "weatherproof," "childproof," "waterproof," "shatterproof," "reinforced," "rock solid," "everlasting," "long-lasting," "indestructible," "sturdy," "reusable," "easily cleanable," and/or "genuine."

Create Attention-Getting Product Listings: A Step-by-Step Guide

One of the core steps in establishing your shop is adding the product listings for the items you plan to sell. You compose and create product listings one at a time, using Etsy®'s "Add a New Listing" tool, which walks you through the process of composing and publishing, and then organizing, each listing. As you're about to discover, Etsy® divides this process into five steps.

▶ Maintain Your Professional Image

Once your shop is open for business, you always have the ability to create, edit, or delete individual product listings. Based on the response you receive from visitors (feedback, questions, complaints, or compliments), you should update your product listings as often as is necessary.

Using your computer, laptop, or the Sell on Etsy® mobile app from your smartphone or tablet, log onto Etsy®, click the Your Shop button, choose the Stock Your Shop option, and then select the Add a New Listing option or click an item listing that already exists (to edit, copy, or delete it).

To achieve the best possible customer response from each product listing, only publish the listing within your shop after the Add a New Listing form has been completed and the information you've written has been properly edited and proofread. Do not take shortcuts or rush this process.

Spelling mistakes, grammatical mistakes, the use of inappropriate or incorrect words, and/or poor use of the English language is unacceptable. Any of these mistakes will quickly tarnish your company and personal reputation by making you look amateurish, uneducated, and unprofessional.

Anytime you want to create a new product listing, click the Add a Listing option that's found on the "Stock Your Shop" screen. Then fill in each field with the appropriate information in the "Add a New Listing" questionnaire screen.

Product Listing Step 1: Product Photography

The first step in creating a product listing involves uploading between one and five digital photos for each listing (shown in Figure 5–1). Take advantage of this and choose five photos that best showcase your products from different angles or perspectives. Mix and match traditional product shots with lifestyle shots.

A product shot depicts just your item in the photo, typically with a white or solid color (or very simple) background. The primary focus should be on the product itself, and it should show as much product detail as possible. One product shot might be taken from a head-on perspective to showcase the entire item. Another shot

tip

More information about how to best showcase your items with photography is covered later in this chapter, so be sure to read the section "How to Take Professional-Quality Product Photos" whether you plan to take your own photos or hire a photographer to take them for you.

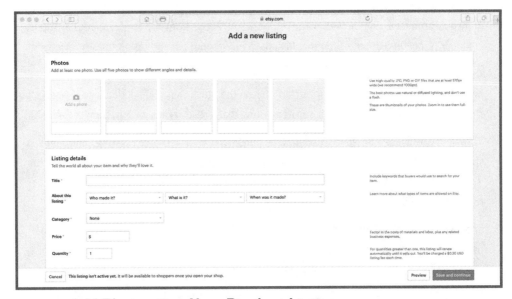

FIGURE 5–1: **Add Photos to a New Product Listing**
You can add up to five separate digital photos to each product listing.

might zoom in to highlight a specific feature or detail the item offers, while other shots could show off the item from different angles or perspectives.

A lifestyle shot captures your product being worn or used in the real world. For example, if you sell necklaces, a lifestyle shot could show a model wearing the necklace in conjunction with work, casual, and/or formal attire.

Product Listing Step 2: Listing Details

One of the very first things a visitor to your shop sees when they view each of your products, in addition to the photography, is the product listing's title. This title must be short, descriptive, attention-getting, accurate, and contain keywords that you believe customers will use to search for your items.

A well-written title will encourage a visitor to invest a few extra minutes to view the entire product listing, or it could just as easily make them want to leave your shop and find similar items elsewhere. You only have a few seconds to capture someone's attention, and the title is one of the most powerful tools for doing this. Think carefully when composing each title. As always, target it specifically to your core audience.

The "About This Listing" section includes three separate pull-down menus (shown in Figure 5–2, page 96): "Who Made It?," "What Is It?," and "When Was It Made?" One at a time, click each pull-down menu and select the most appropriate option based on what you're selling.

Next, choose just one applicable category for the product. Your options include:

- ▶ Accessories
- ▶ Art & Collectibles
- ▶ Bags & Purses
- ▶ Bath & Beauty
- ▶ Books, Movies, and Music
- ▶ Clothing
- ▶ Craft Supplies & Tools
- ▶ Electronics & Accessories
- ▶ Home & Living
- ▶ Jewelry
- ▶ Paper & Party Supplies
- ▶ Pet Supplies
- ▶ Shoes
- ▶ Toys & Games
- ▶ Weddings

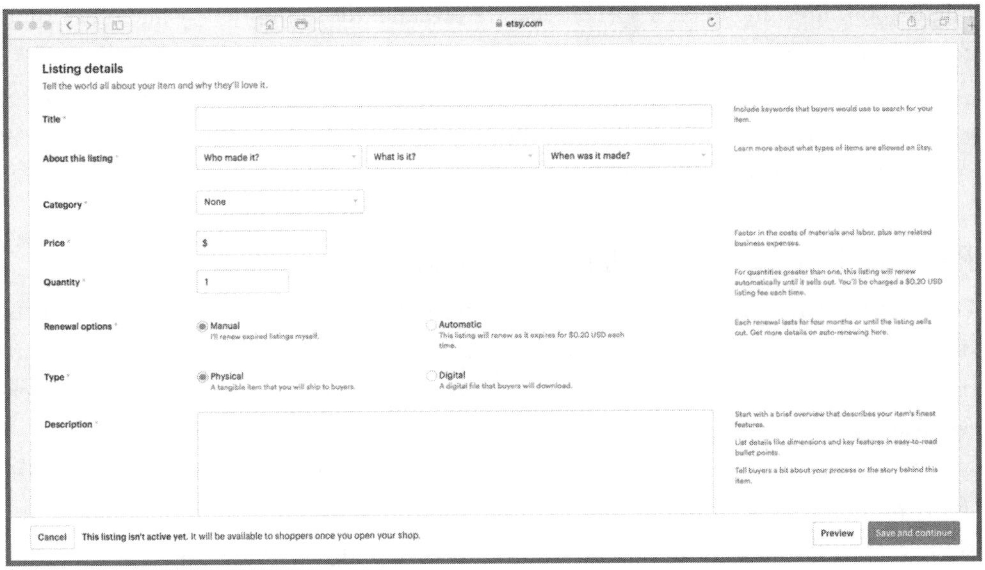

FIGURE 5–2: **About This Listing Options**

This allows you to provide additional information about your product by selecting appropriate responses from pull-down menus.

After selecting a category, fill in the Price field with the cost of your item. This price should be precalculated to take into account your cost of materials, time/labor, business overhead expenses, and marketing/advertising expenses, as well as the profit you want to earn. It should not include the shipping and handling fee or sales tax unless you want to include these for free for your customer and not charge these fees separately.

Now enter the number of a single item you have available to sell in the Quantity field. If you have an unlimited supply, because you make the item yourself, for example, enter a quantity of 10 or 25. You don't want it to appear that you have hundreds of the item in stock and nobody is buying it. Remember, you can always relist the item. In most cases, you're better off showing that the item's supply is somewhat limited to create a sense of urgency for the customer to make a purchase.

Because each listing will only remain active for up to four months (or until the item sells out), you can manually or automatically relist the item by clicking on the appropriate option in the Renewal field.

For the Type option, choose between physical or digital. If the item is tangible and it will ultimately be shipping to the buyers, then it's a physical item. However, if the item is a digital file that the buyer will immediately download once their purchase it made, then it's a digital item.

The Description field is an important part of every product listing. This is where you can use freeform text to describe your product using your own words. Use as many relevant search words or phrases as you can because the content of this text will be searchable by your potential customers. Again, keep your descriptions informative, attention-getting, accurate, upbeat, and concise. Use this as an opportunity to answer some or all of the questions that were posed earlier in this chapter.

The final part of the "Listing Details" section allows you to sort and display the product listing you're currently creating into a section within your shop. (This is done after the listings are created.) As you learned from the previous chapter, if you are selling multiple items that fit into clearly definable categories, seriously consider using sections to sort your items and make them easier to find within your shop.

tip

The more individual items you plan to showcase in your shop, the more specialized sections you might want to include. If you offer only five different items, there's probably no need for more than one or two sections. However, if you list hundreds of different items in your shop, having 5 or 10 separate sections will typically make sense.

If you're a jewelry maker, for example, sections within your shop might be labeled "Bracelets," "Rings," "Necklaces," and "Earrings." You can also create special sections that showcase groups of items for specific audiences, such as "Gifts for Him," "Gifts for Her," "Gifts for Brides," "Gifts for New Moms," "Gifts for Recent Grads."

Another option is to sort your products based on pricing. For example, sections might include: "Gifts Under $100," "Gifts Under $50," or "Gifts Under $25." If you want to showcase specific items that make the perfect gift for an upcoming holiday, additional sections might include: "Perfect Mother's Day Gifts," "Christmas Gifts," or "Holiday Items."

A special section for "Last Chance Sale Items," "Soon to Be Discontinued Items," or "Seasonal Items" can also be included in your shop. The good news is you're able to create as many separate sections as you desire in your shop. However, you want to make your items easy to find, so avoid offering too many choices that will ultimately make it confusing for your visitors.

If you haven't already set up different sections within your shop, click on the Add Your First Section option to create each section and give it a unique title. Then, once you've created one or more sections, a pull-down menu will appear, allowing you to select which section a new product listing should be included under.

Keep in mind, even if you create multiple sections, you always have the option to display one or more items without associating them with a specific section. To do this, select the None option from the Section pull-down menu when creating or editing a product listing.

Product Listing Step 3: Variations

If you were operating a traditional retail store, every item (or item variation) you offer would display a separate and unique UPC barcode on its packaging. For example, the small blue widget would have a different UPC barcode than the medium green widget. On Etsy®, however, a single product listing for an individual item can have multiple (optional) variations.

For example, the "Handmade Wool Sweater" you're selling could have one listing, and using the Add a Variation tool, the listing could offer the sweater in multiple colors and/or sizes that you choose to offer. Once you activate the Variations option, every customer is then required to choose from one of the Variation options when placing their order.

The Variation option(s) that the customer selects will be displayed on your Sold Orders, Receipts, and Transaction emails, so you'll know exactly what item(s) to send based on the customer's choices.

Following are variation options (shown in Figure 5–3, page 99) you can choose to offer:

- ▶ Color
- ▶ Device
- ▶ Diameter
- ▶ Dimensions
- ▶ Fabric
- ▶ Finish
- ▶ Flavor
- ▶ Height
- ▶ Length
- ▶ Material
- ▶ Pattern
- ▶ Scent
- ▶ Size

warning

When creating the variations for each product listing, keep it simple. Don't force the customer to make too many complicated decisions. For example, if you're offering the same bracelet in 10k gold, 14k gold, 24k gold, silver, and platinum, and each option is available in five or more different sizes, and/or with one or more additional customer-selectable options (such as engraving, etc.), consider creating separate product listings for each metal type. Doing this will make it easier to showcase each option in your product photos and make choosing less confusing for the customer as they're placing an order.

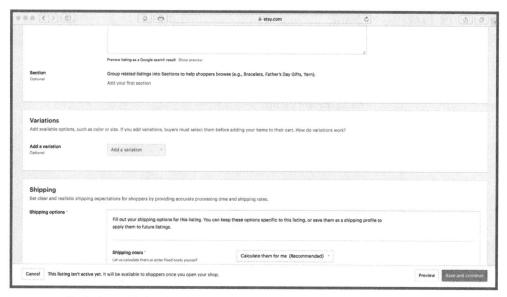

FIGURE 5–3: **Select a Variation**

▶ Style
▶ Weight
▶ Width
▶ Add a New Property

Once you select a variation, customize what options your customers will be given based on the type of variation you select.

Based on the variation option you choose for your product listing, you'll be prompted with additional questions to select the most applicable options. For example, if you select the Size Variation, you'll be asked, "What scale are your sizes in?" You'll be asked to choose between Alpha, Inches, Centimeters, Fluid Ounces, Milliliters, Liters, or Other.

If you plan to offer the item in small, medium, large, and extra-large, for example, select the Other option, and then in the Add an Option field, enter each size label to be offered, one at a time, clicking on the Add button after each size option.

With each variation that you select and apply, you have the option of adding a separate price and displaying whether that particular variation option is currently in stock. By default, all items within a particular product listing will display the price you previously assigned to it. However, if you opt to charge a premium for a large or extra-large size, for example, you can update the price for these variations by clicking the Add Pricing option.

Product Listing Step 4: Shipping Details

This section of the product listing requires you to provide details about the size and weight of your item and where it will be shipping from; select the shipping options you want to offer to your customers; and disclose the processing time needed to fill each order.

One at a time, fill in the field for each option. For the Shipping Costs option (shown in Figure 5–4), Etsy® recommends that you choose the Calculate Them for Me option. To learn more about how this works, visit: www.Etsy.com/help/article/6131. The alternative is to manually enter your fixed shipping costs for each item.

Next, provide the origin zip code for the location you will be shipping your orders from.

Click on the Processing Time option to set how long it will typically take you to create and fulfill an

tip

If you want to offer free domestic shipping or free international shipping, add a checkmark to the appropriate checkbox displayed to the right of the Free Shipping option. If you build flat rate USPS priority shipping into your item's price, and then offer free domestic shipping, that's an option your domestic customers will likely appreciate, assuming this doesn't dramatically increase the price of your item.

FIGURE 5–4: **Setting Shipping Information for Your Etsy® Shop**
Provide all the requested information about the shipping options you want to offer and what you will be shipping, and allow Etsy® to calculate your shipping prices.

order once it's been placed. As a general rule, offer the fastest processing time possible. Choose the One Business Day or One to Two Business Days option if you can adhere to this. The only exception to this is if an item is being custom made and it takes you several days or weeks to create that item to the customer's specifications from scratch.

Select what countries you'll ship orders to in the Where I'll Ship box. Keep in mind that the customer will pay for the international shipping charges, but you may be required to fill out extra paperwork in conjunction with each shipment to ship your item(s) abroad. The default option for this setting is United States and Worldwide. Click on the Edit option that's displayed to the right of the Where I'll Ship option if you want to change this setting. Otherwise, proceed to the Shipping Services option.

Assuming you're based in the United States, the default option for Shipping Services (which the buyer will be able to choose from at checkout) includes six United States Postal Service Classes (USPS Priority Mail, USPS Priority Mail Express, USPS First Class Package Services, USPS Priority Mail International, and USPS Priority Mail Express International). Additional USPS shipping options you can optionally add include: USPS Media Mail and USPS Parcel Select Ground.

Based on the shipping option(s) you choose to offer and the option that the customer selects when placing an order, Etsy® will calculate the shipping/postage fee based on current rates. You have the option to offer Free Domestic Shipping or Free International Shipping to your customers, which means that the shipping fees must be paid by you and will not be added to the buyer's order subtotal when they're making a purchase.

In addition to the shipping charges that Etsy® will calculate based on current rates, you have the option to add a handling fee that your customers will need to pay when placing their order. This fee will be automatically added to the customer's shipping total and will not be listed separately. A handling fee may cover costs for the shipping materials (box, packing tape, etc.) needed to ship your item, as well as the time it takes you to process and fill the order. Adding a handling fee is optional for sellers. If you choose to add one, keep it low and be able

warning ⚠

International shipping charges are typically high. If you opt to include free international shipping and build these fees into your price, you will have to increase your price significantly, which will make it appear less competitive from a pricing standpoint. If your customers are located within a different country, they'll understand that additional international shipping charges will apply. Think twice about offering free international shipping, or you could see your profit margin disappear!

to justify it. For example, if your customer knows it will cost you $10 to ship the item to them using the selected shipping method, but they're being charged a $25 shipping and handling fee, they might resent this and choose to shop elsewhere, causing you to lose a sale.

Once you've provided responses to each of the options within the Shipping section of a product listing, click Save as a Shipping Profile if you want to be able to use identical settings as you create additional product listings.

Next, provide the item weight (in pounds and ounces) for the item you will be shipping after it's been packaged. In the Item Size (when packed) fields, also supply the length, width, and height of the package that you're planning to ship. Based on the various shipping options you've selected, in the Preview Shipping Costs field, Etsy® will display what your customers will be charged for shipping and handling when placing an order.

Product Listing Step 5: Add Search Terms

The final step in the product listing process may seem quick and easy, but it's also something you want to put a lot of advance thought into. The up to 13 individual words you add to the Tags field will help customers find your shop and product listing when using the Etsy® search tool or an internet search engine. As a result, the up to 13 tags you provide should accurately describe your item in the most detailed way possible.

Try to anticipate the exact words that a potential customer would type into a search field in order to find what you're selling. Be as specific as you can, again keeping your target customer in mind. Separate each Tag you add to the Tags field with a comma.

The Materials field is another optional tool you can use to provide a collection of search words that you think potential customers might use to locate your product online. It's displayed during the listing creation process, when applicable, and provides a list of what's used to make the item, each separated by a comma. You're allowed to provide up to 13 words within the Materials field. For example, if you're selling a handmade sweater, your materials list might include words such as "wool," "yarn," "all-natural," "organic," "died," "handspun," "synthetic," "Scottish," "Merino," "sheep," "alpaca," "cashmere," and/or "natural."

aha!

Need ideas for what tags to use? Consider words that describe specifically what the item is, who the item is for, what color it comes in, how it was made, what size it comes in, what style it offers, and/or what material it's made from. Also, think about commonly used synonyms for the tags you initially select.

Once you've completed a product listing and have provided all the information requested, click the Preview button to view exactly how the listing will appear in your shop.

As you're viewing a preview, proofread everything, and make sure all the text, photos, price, and variations, for example, are correct. If you need to fix or change anything, click on the Continue Editing button to edit the listing. Otherwise, click the Save and continue button to store and publish the listing in your shop.

You can also click just Save and continue and not Preview to store and publish the listing within your shop button, too, but this is not recommended.

How to Take Professional-Quality Product Photos

It's been said that a single picture is worth a 1,000 words. Well, because Etsy® allows you to showcase up to five pictures per product listing, you're given the opportunity to quickly and visually convey a lot of useful information to prospective customers, plus use photography to create a need or want for whatever it is you're selling.

In addition to using skillfully written, flowery, and sales-oriented prose to explain exactly what you're selling, put a lot of attention and emphasis on your photos. Whatever equipment and approach you use to take your photos, at the very least, the images should be well-lit, crystal-clear, shadow-free, and nicely depict your item(s), without any visual distractions.

It's been proven over and over again on Etsy® that the more professional-looking your photos are, the better chances you have of making a sale. That being said, you have several options for acquiring the product photos you need:

▶ Hire a professional (or semi-professional) photographer, with experience in product photography, to take your photos. This will probably cost you money upfront, but you should think of this as a worthwhile investment in the future success of your business.

▶ Purchase a good-quality, high-resolution digital camera (at least 12-megapixel resolution, although the higher the resolution, the better), along with a professional-quality lighting setup, tripod, and lightbox (or backgrounds) to take your own photos. This will cost you anywhere

aha!

When you visit other Etsy® shops to do your research, study the photography and determine what you like and what approaches you believe work best. While you don't want to blatantly copy someone else's photos, you should definitely use them for creative inspiration and to help you define your own picture quality standards.

from several hundred to several thousand dollars. Companies such as Adorama (www.adorama.com) and B&H Photo/Video (www.bhphotovideo.com) sell all the photo equipment you will need. You'll also find discounted cameras, lighting, lightboxes, and related equipment sold on Amazon and eBay.

▶ Use the camera that's built into your smartphone. The latest model Apple iPhones and Android smartphones have a good-quality, rear-facing camera built in. When used in conjunction with appropriate lighting and a lightbox, for example, you can typically achieve really good results with a minimal financial investment.

When taking your lifestyle photos, you can recruit your friends or family members to be models or contact a local modeling agency in your city and hire professional models who have the specific look you need to showcase photos that will appeal to your target audience. Model Mayhem (www.modelmayhem.com) is an online service that can be used for finding and hiring aspiring or professional models in the United States. You can use the service's search tool to find models that have a specific look and who meet your criteria.

warning

Do not ever "borrow" or outright steal photography from other Etsy® shops or online sources. Unless you obtain written permission to use someone else's photography, this is considered copyright infringement and could easily result in legal action being taken against you.

While you have the option to purchase stock photography from an online service, such as iStockPhoto (www.istockphoto.com), Shutterstock (www.shutterstock.com), or Adobe Stock (https://stock.adobe.com), this will not be original artwork. You're better off showcasing original and exclusive images of your items in your Etsy® store.

tip

The online *Etsy® Seller Handbook* is chock-full of how-to articles and information that will help you take professional-quality photos of your items or hire the best photographer for the job (without spending a fortune). To find these articles, visit: www.Etsy.com/seller-handbook/category/photography.

As you begin creating or editing a product listing, you're allowed to upload up to five photos per listing. Each photo must be saved in a .jpg, .png, or .gif digital file format. Once you've taken and edited your images, click the Add a Photo option located near the top of the "Add a Listing" page to upload each image and include it in a product listing.

► Use a Lightbox for Product Photography

One of the best tools you can use to take consistently good-quality product photos, with a solid color background, especially if the items you're photographing are rather small, is a tabletop lightbox (also sometimes referred to as a light tent).

This photography tool is used in conjunction with lights (often sold separately). A lightbox can be used with the camera built into your smartphone, a point-and-shoot digital camera, or a high-end digital SLR camera, for example.

A lightbox is square-shaped, typically fits on a tabletop, and is made from white, translucent material that ultimately gets surrounded by external lights. The lightbox allows the item you're photographing to be surrounded by a soft, even light, without harsh shadows or unwanted glares being created.

Depending on the size lightbox you need and whether specialized photography lights are included in the package, you can shop online and find a tabletop lightbox priced between $50 and $350. To find lightboxes online, visit Amazon, eBay, Adorama, or B&H Photo/Video, for example, and in the search field, enter "lightbox."

Many Etsy® sellers are able to invest less than $100 in a lightbox and lighting and use the camera built into their smartphone to capture decent quality product photos, which can then be edited and enhanced using a photo editing mobile app or computer software.

Instead of using a lightbox, many Etsy® sellers have achieved success taking their product shots outdoors against a solid color or simple background, using natural lighting. Avoid using the camera's flash, or you'll often wind up with unwanted shadows, glares, or reflections in the image or an overexposed image that drowns out the true colors and detail of the product you're trying to showcase.

If you're not willing or able to take your own product shots and achieve really good, professional-looking results, hire someone to help you because the quality of your products shots goes a long way toward building a positive first impression with customers and play a huge role in their purchasing decision when shopping on Etsy®.

Taking professional-quality lifestyle photos is a lot more difficult for amateur or inexperienced photographers who don't have the proper equipment. If utilizing this type of shot in your shop will be beneficial, again, seriously consider hiring a professional photographer to help you.

▶ **Use a Lightbox for Product Photography,** continued

A less expensive alternative to hiring a professional photographer is to contact a local college or university that has a recognized photography program and offer a paid or unpaid internship opportunity to a student who is looking to expand their portfolio. You might also consider finding a friend or family member who is a photography enthusiast and who already owns the equipment you need, and ask that person to help you shoot the photos you need as a favor.

12 Tips for Taking Great Product Photos

The following 12 tips will help you take better quality photos, assuming you're using the appropriate equipment, and take advantage of your own creativity to frame and edit your shots:

1. Be sure to keep your product photos consistent across your shop. Use the same colored background in your images, or at least stick with the same color scheme that you've already used to help establish and define your brand.

2. For traditional product shots, keep your background simple and refrain from including anything in the photo that could distract the viewer from the item detail you're trying to showcase.

3. Make sure the lighting evenly shines on your item so it's well-lit and clearly visible within the photo(s). You want to capture as much detail as possible.

4. Take product shots from different angles and shooting perspectives so that you depict the item you're selling from all sides.

5. When applicable, zoom in and emphasize a specific detail or feature of your item. For example, the intricate nature of the stitching, the detail of the buttons, or the durability of the clasp or zipper.

6. Particularly for small items, place a familiar object in the photo to help demonstrate your item's size. For example, use a quarter or a pen.

7. Always use a tripod when taking product shots, especially if you're using the zoom feature of your camera. This will keep the camera still so your shots won't turn out blurry due to camera movement.

8. When creating lifestyle photos, depict your product in use but stick with familiar situations that your customer will relate to. Keep the images as simple and straightforward as possible, and try to tell a story with each image.

9. When editing and enhancing your photos, take advantage of the crop tool to reframe your shots, as needed, and then use the sharpen tool to boost the clarity of the images. Take advantage of the saturation tool to make the colors in your images more vivid. If you choose to feature your images in black and white, this is a creative decision that can be used in some situations to provide a more artsy aesthetic to your shop. This only works, however, if color does not play an important role in the appearance of your item.

10. Take advantage of the depth of field to focus on your item and blur the background (aka the bokeh effect), to place more visual emphasis on what you're selling and to make

tip

If one shot type doesn't apply to your item, use two or three different variations of the shots that do apply. However, showcase the five images you're allowed to, and make sure each image serves a purpose and contributes something to the overall product listing.

▶ Other Ways Photos Can Be Used in Your Shop

In addition to the product shots that accompany each product listing, you have the ability to add original photography on your shop's main page, as well as in the "About" section and your personal profile.

These images should showcase your products but also help establish and communicate your company's brand and tell your story. For example, in your shop's "About" section, include photos of your workshop, your items being created, your creative process, what inspires you, your specialized tools, and you (or your artists) at work. These can be a combination of candid and posed photos, but they should all be taken by a professional photographer, or look professional, not like a selfie shot with your smartphone.

These photos, along with your own profile photo, can help humanize your company, differentiate you from your competition, and draw in your potential customers so that they relate more to what you're offering, understand your inspiration, and feel compelled by your story to support your business by becoming a customer.

You'll discover that buyers on Etsy® often want to become part of something they deem as special and want to support the sellers that they personally relate to the most.

the photos look more interesting. Remember, the item you're selling must always appear in focus.

11. Use the white balance feature of your camera, if applicable, to ensure the colors captured in your images are authentic and accurate. You can also use the white balance tool found in most photo editing software packages to accomplish this.

12. Keeping in mind you have five photos to fully show off each item, here are the types of shots to consider:

   ▶ At least one traditional product shot with a solid-color (or simple) background that shows the front of the product.

   ▶ A similar traditional product shot taken from a different angle (to showcase the side or back of the item, or that allows the item to be seen from a different perspective).

   ▶ One shot that zooms in on your product to show its detail.

   ▶ One shot that demonstrates the size of the item by also including a familiar item (such as a coin) that people know the size of.

   ▶ One lifestyle shot that shows off the product in use in the real world. These shots should demonstrate some creativity and be visually interesting while being informative for the viewer.

Meet Jane Katirgis, Co-Proprietor of Elegance Farm Homestead

Featured on their Etsy® Store (Figure 5–5, page 109) Elegance Farm Homestead (www.Etsy.com/shop/EleganceFarmHome), are the creations of Jane Katirgis and her husband John—customized and handcrafted magnetic bulletin boards and framed magnetic chalkboards that are suitable for in-home or office use. These items are available in a wide range of sizes and designs that can be made to match almost any décor.

In this interview, Jane shares her experience using Etsy® to operate her business. Her first exposure to Etsy® was several years ago when she established a small shop through which she sold bookmarks. "This was a fun little hobby, but it allowed me to familiarize myself with the Etsy® platform and learn how to operate a business using this service. For example, I learned the importance of having really high-quality product photos displayed within a store," she says.

It was a bit later that Jane and her husband came up with the idea to create handcrafted magnetic bulletin boards with customized frames. "The idea came as a result of a request from a relative. My husband made the first bulletin board as a gift, and I thought it

FIGURE 5–5: **The Main Page of Elegance Farm Homestead's Etsy® Shop**

was really pretty and very unique. We photographed the item, and I stuck it up online in my first Etsy® shop. Almost immediately, it generated a lot of interest and a strong response, so we created a separate Etsy® store for these wood-framed magnetic bulletin board products," recalls Jane. "We now custom build these items in different sizes and in a variety of styles."

For one year, starting in February of 2011, Jane and John ran this Etsy® shop on a part-time basis, and both held full-time jobs. "It got to the point where we could not both have a full-time job and run the Etsy® business, so we made a decision and made running our Elegant Farm Home business our full-time jobs," says Jane. "We both decided at the same time to leave our other full-time jobs back in the spring of 2012."

Jane originally learned about Etsy® from a friend. "I checked out the Etsy® website and was immediately captivated by the visual look for the service itself, as well as the way that each shop was able to have its own look and tell its unique story. On other services, a seller cannot customize the look of their shop as well as the appearance of each product listing. I really liked the look and feel of Etsy® and found that it was very easy to get started using the service," says Jane.

"As your business, your brand, and your products evolve, it's necessary for the look and content within your Etsy® shop to evolve as well. The ability to give your shop a custom look gives you the ability to customize it in a way that will truly showcase whatever it is you're selling and at the same time, cater the information directly to your target audience in a way that will appeal to them.

"Our products are high-end because we custom build each frame to order. Our customer base is comprised of upper-middle-class to upper-class people who have money to spend on luxury items," says Jane. "It wasn't until we really started selling our products that we were able to learn a lot about our customers. Back when I started using Etsy® to sell bookmarks, I opened the shop on a whim and had no preconceptions about what to expect. However, when my husband and I opened the Elegance Farm Homestead business, I had a much better idea about how the Etsy® service worked and what we could expect from it."

After launching Elegance Farm Homestead on Etsy®, Jane and John took a close look at other similar services, including Amazon, but found that the percentage of each sale that Etsy® charges was much more reasonable than the service's competition. "We receive a lot of customers from Etsy®'s established community of buyers, and that alone is worth the percentage of each sale that the service charges its sellers. We have looked into starting our own ecommerce website, but we honestly have not had the time to pursue this. Plus, we are really pleased with Etsy®," Jane adds.

When the couple decided to open Elegance Farm Homestead on Etsy®, they invested about 40 hours to customize their Etsy® store and get everything in working order. It took additional time to create the initial inventory of products that were showcased in the shop. "We took the time we needed to carefully create each product listing, take high-quality product photos, and consider our pricing for each item. Then, once the shop was open and live, we continued to tweak everything on an ongoing basis. For example, based on initial customer questions, I updated our product listings to answer the most common questions so customers would not have to contact us to get answers to those questions," explains Jane.

The initial financial investment to launch Elegance Farm Homestead was minimal for Jane and John Katirgis because they already had all the woodworking tools they needed to create their products. "We invested several hundred dollars in materials to create our initial inventory. I think one reason why we were successful is that we did not spend too much money upfront. We didn't take out a loan, for example, to fund the business initially. We started out small with what we had and then slowly built on that. Once we started earning money, we upgraded some of our equipment, for example," says Jane.

Once the Etsy® store launched, Jane recalls it took about two weeks before Elegance Farm Homestead received its first sale. "The sales were slow at first. After our first sale, it was two weeks before the next sale. The following week, we then had one or two sales, and the pace slowly picked up. In the meantime, we kept photographing and uploading new pieces to showcase in the store. My goal was to keep increasing the number of items displayed in the shop because I think it's important for a shop to offer a bunch of different items—not just three or four. Potential customers want items to choose from, and by displaying a bunch of items, it makes your shop look more substantial," adds Jane.

If she were to start all over again, knowing what she knows now, Jane would launch a new Etsy® shop with higher-quality product photos than they initially had. "Etsy® is a very visual-oriented platform, and having really good product photos, I believe, is the most important aspect of an Etsy® store. I look back at our initial product photos and realize they were dark, grainy, did not utilize natural light, and shot from really bad angles. Looking back, I would have started out with better quality photographs. As a seller, you need a potential customer to notice your product photos instantly and want to click on the listing. If your photos don't capture someone's attention, you will lose sales."

Beyond having the highest quality photos possible, Jane recommends that a seller really utilize tags and keywords to make their items easily searchable and locatable on the Etsy® platform.

"Etsy® also offers paid ads, which provide a way to help sellers get noticed among Etsy®'s established customer base. We have not needed to use these ads yet because we have been getting so many orders that we periodically need to close the shop temporarily to catch up and fill the outstanding orders we have.

"From speaking with other Etsy® sellers, however, the paid Etsy® advertising does seem to really work for some stores. I also recommend that sellers really take advantage of the SEO tools that the Etsy® platform offers. If you use these tools correctly, and the best possible selection of keywords and tags, it makes it much easier for potential customer to find your store, whether they're using Etsy®'s search tool or a popular search engine, like Google," says Jane.

Below the name of every Etsy® shop, sellers can use up to seven keywords or tags to identify and describe their shop. Choosing the most appropriate selection of words is important. "For our business, displayed directly below our store name are our SEO words, which include 'Magnet,' 'Bulletin Board,' 'Frames,' 'Fabric,' and 'Chalkboard.' Built into the Etsy® site are a selection of online resources that new sellers can use to learn about SEO, for example," she adds.

One area Jane has discovered Etsy® to be lacking is when it comes to setting shipping prices. "Setting your shipping prices is something you, as a seller, need to research on your own based on what you're selling and how you want to ship your items to your customers when filling orders. Do your research based on what you'll be shipping so you know in advance how much to charge your customers," Jane explains.

Like so many other successful Etsy® sellers, Jane and John spend between one and four hours per day answering emails from prospective and existing customers. On average, each puts in a full 40-hour work week each and every week, although a lot of additional time is required during the peak holiday season.

"Right now, we don't have the need to do a lot of marketing or advertising. All our customers find us on the Etsy® service, learn about us through word-of-mouth from existing customers, or we receive repeat orders from existing customers," Jane says. "At this point, we don't have the time to take on additional work, so doing a lot of additional marketing or advertising would not be too beneficial, unless we wanted to begin working an 80-hour week, hire employees, and move to a larger work space. I know there are some great ways to market an Etsy® business that will generate more customers, but this is luckily something we have not had to do as of yet. In the future, I hope to start an online newsletter or blog as a way to keep in touch with our customers."

One reason why Elegance Farm Homestead has become successful, despite having some competition, is because Jane and John handcraft all their own wooden frames for their products from scratch. Doing this allows them to custom-build any size a customer requests. "More than half our orders are for a custom-size bulletin board or chalkboard. Our customers appreciate something that's handmade and well made and are willing to pay a premium price for what they're receiving," says Jane.

According to Jane, her company's pricing is based on the cost of materials, the time it takes to make a piece, and what they believe they should earn as a fair hourly wage for their work to support themselves. They have chosen not to sell their products wholesale, so the commonly used formula of time and materials times two to set a wholesale price, and then doubling that to set a retail price, doesn't really apply to them.

"If we followed that formula exactly, our prices would be higher than they are because of the time it takes to make each piece. As a result, our retail prices are a bit lower than what they'd be if we followed that formula, but in the scheme of things, they're still what you'd consider to be premium prices," adds Jane. "Our products look nothing like the dry-erase boards, bulletin boards, or chalkboards you'd buy at Staples or Office Max, for example. We have received orders from very large companies asking for massive, custom dry erase boards for their conference rooms."

Based on what it's selling, Elegance Farm Homestead would never be able to exist as a successful business if it were operated from a traditional brick and mortar retail store that needed to be staffed by employees and remain open during predefined business hours.

"We could not sustain paying that overhead and could never make a living. Thus, operating an Etsy® store provides us with a business opportunity that would not otherwise be possible. Etsy® is very shopper-friendly and is a wonderful platform to use as a seller. If I actually think about it, absolutely nothing jumps out in my mind if I try to think of something that's bad about Etsy® that I would want to warn potential sellers about," says Jane. "Anytime I have ever had any type of glitch or question, I have been able to email Etsy® directly and receive a very prompt response, which, as a seller, is very comforting."

While Jane believes it's important to give potential and existing customers the option to either call or email a shop owner, she admits that in any given month, they may receive just one phone call.

"Almost everyone prefers to contact us via email with their questions. However, I think potential customers are comforted by the fact that they could call us if they wanted to or if they had a genuine problem," adds Jane. "Because we custom make each order, one of the most common questions we receive is how long it will take us to fill a new order. Whenever I receive a question via email, I always take the time to respond with a friendly, well-thought-out, and personalized reply."

One additional piece of advice that Jane offers to first-time Etsy® sellers is that they should regularly update their shop and make an effort to keep their content and appearance fresh.

She adds, "Make sure you register your business with your state, that you pay your taxes, and use specialized accounting and bookkeeping software to manage your company finances. Also, consider investing in business insurance, if this is something you'll benefit from."

For people who are thinking about launching their own Etsy® store, Jane suggests that you choose to do something that you really love, because if it does take off, you'll want to really like what you're doing. "Also, don't try to grow your business too quickly. Be practical and make intelligent and well-thought-out business decisions. In a way, I think we got a bit lucky in that we filled a void for products that people want, that there is a demand for, and that we really love to create.

Concludes Jane, "Once you begin running your Etsy® business, earning five-star ratings and reviews from your customers is a lot more important than your store having a lot of admirers. Do whatever is necessary to earn the best possible reviews, keeping in mind that the majority of your customers will not leave a review, even if they absolutely love the product you sold them. Whatever you do, don't nag or pester your customers to leave a review."

Additional Thoughts

Hopefully, you now understand the importance or creating detailed and well written product descriptions in addition to providing the best possible product photography with each listing. These are not areas where you want to cut corners. Having an awesome product that's promoted poorly or in an unprofessional manner within your shop will prove to be a huge mistake. Once your shop is open for business, your next focus needs to be on driving a constant flow of traffic to your shop. The next chapter's focus is on marketing and advertising your product(s) and your business.

Promoting and Marketing Your Etsy® Shop

Perhaps the most common misconception first-time Etsy® sellers have when they launch their own shop can be summed up with the phrase, "If you build it, they will come." Unfortunately, this is simply not the case with an Etsy® shop or any other online business for that matter. Creating and launching an Etsy® shop is only the first step.

Now, as the shop owner, it becomes your ongoing responsibility to continuously do marketing and potentially paid advertising for your shop and your products to drive a steady flow of traffic to your shop. In fact, moving forward, a good chunk of the time you spend managing your business will probably be spent handling marketing and advertising activities.

This chapter describes some of the more commonly used marketing and advertising tools, resources, and opportunities available to you. Which ones you choose to implement will depend on what you're selling, who you have defined as your target audience and how much time and money you have available.

Before proceeding with any of these activities, however, be sure that you have already developed a thorough understanding of who comprises your Etsy® shop's target audience, and that you've defined a clear and concise message about your shop and your products that you want to convey to this audience.

Your Marketing and Advertising Should Be Consistent with Your Brand

All the marketing and advertising you do in conjunction with your business should complement and promote your brand. Your brand is the identity you've established for your business to help you stand out from the competition.

For example, your brand includes your company logo, color scheme, marketing slogan, core marketing message, the company philosophy you're trying to promote, the selection of products you choose to sell, and your reputation that you build among your customers (which on Etsy® is showcased in part with your ratings and reviews).

As a general strategy, you want your marketing and advertising efforts to be synergistic with your brand, share the same core marketing message, and be targeted to the same core target audience.

There's a Difference Between Marketing and Advertising

Marketing refers to the activities you do online or in the real world that cost little or no money but that allow you to promote your Etsy® shop and drive traffic to it. Examples of marketing efforts you might adopt include becoming active on social media, participating in real-world crafts fairs, promoting your Etsy® shop and products by starting a blog or newsletter related to your shop and what you sell, or utilizing a public relations campaign in hopes of generating free publicity in the media about your Etsy® shop and products.

Marketing campaigns tend to require time and effort to plan and execute but cost very little or no money upfront, which makes them very attractive to startup businesses.

Advertising refers to the paid opportunities available to promote your business online or in the real world. Examples of paid advertising that tend to work very well for Etsy® sellers include Facebook advertising, Google AdWords advertising, and Etsy® advertising. You can also run ads in specialty interest publications or media that relate directly to what you're selling and that reach your core target audience.

In addition to time, effort, and some level of expertise to plan and execute, paid advertising campaigns cost money that you'll need to invest upfront to reap the benefits. You'll discover that some ad campaigns will work better than others based on what you're selling. However, if you don't properly target your ad campaign, or you use the wrong approach in your campaign, you'll spend money but won't achieve the desired results. Thus, it's essential that you learn all about the paid advertising method you choose before investing your money to use it.

Reach Etsy®'s Community of Buyers

The good news is that Etsy® has an established, vast, and ever-growing customer base that visits Etsy® whenever they want to shop for the types of items that typically are sold on this platform. This does not guarantee those shoppers will visit your store, however.

To increase the chances that Etsy® shoppers will find you, it's essential that you utilize Etsy®'s SEO tools so you come up in search results. You also have the option of using paid Etsy® advertising so your products get featured online.

Even if you fully utilize these two options, visitors will likely only trickle to your shop. It ultimately becomes your responsibility to utilize other marketing and advertising approaches to drive a steadier flow of traffic to it. Then it's up to the content you've incorporated into your shop to convert that traffic into paying customers.

tip ⓘ

To achieve the best marketing and advertising results, adopt a multifaceted approach to your efforts. Instead of focusing all your time, money, and effort on just one marketing or advertising strategy or campaign, you should always have at least three separate campaigns running to ensure you're reaching the most people within your target audience with the resources you're dedicating to the task.

Popular Marketing Activities You Can Adopt for Your Etsy® Business

This section focuses on some of the commonly used marketing activities you can adopt for your business. Which options you choose are entirely up to you and should be based on your available resources, your target audience, and what items you'll be selling.

Bear in mind that marketing efforts don't always have an instantaneous result. Sometimes, you'll need to wait a few weeks or even several months before you start reaping the benefits of your efforts and see increased traffic to your Etsy® shop.

While many of the available marketing efforts may seem exciting to you, some require a learning curve, and others take time to properly implement. Be sure you don't overwhelm yourself with too many responsibilities as you first launch your Etsy® shop, or you could wind up becoming frustrated and overworked, and ultimately make costly mistakes.

Word-of-Mouth Works Best

If you're able to impress your customers, get them excited about what you're offering, and provide top-notch customer service, one of your rewards as a seller is that they may speak favorably about you among their friends, coworkers, and family members. Plus, if your customers become loyal to you and what you're selling, they may also provide a positive endorsement to these people about your company and products.

▶ Word-of-Mouth Publicity Can Have a Negative Result, Too

Word-of-mouth publicity from customers can also have a negative impact on your company's reputation and sales. If a customer becomes disgruntled for whatever reason, they'll often be inclined to quickly share their complaints and harsh criticism via social media even before addressing that complaint with you, the seller.

This is one reason why it's important to solicit feedback from your customers during every step of the selling and order fulfilment process and to make yourself readily available to address questions and concerns via email or telephone. A personalized and prompt response to a simple issue from you could mean the difference between favorable and unfavorable word-of-mouth publicity.

Because the average person who is active on social media tends to have hundreds of friends, followers, or contacts, a single mention on a customer's Facebook, Twitter, or Instagram feed can either help you, if favorable, or hurt you, if negative.

An even greater reward is that some of your customers may be inclined to share information about you and your company through their social media, which could quickly reach a much larger audience. When you receive complimentary calls or emails from customers, be sure to quickly thank them and politely ask for a favorable review on Etsy® and to tell their friends via social media.

Positive word-of-mouth serves as a reliable endorsement and can be more powerful than any advertisement that someone sees because they know and trust the source of the endorsement, whether it's from a friend, coworker, or family member.

Focus on Generating Repeat Business from Existing Customers

Once you discover how much time, effort, and potentially money goes into driving traffic to your shop, and then see what's involved when it comes to converting that traffic into paying customers, you'll realize that generating repeat business from already satisfied customers is much easier and requires far less effort.

Maintaining communication and a favorable relationship with your customers is one of the easiest ways to generate repeat business. However, you can help to ensure repeat business by adopting several approaches. The one thing you never want to do, however, is harass an existing customer.

Some of the tactics you can use to help generate repeat business and maintain communication with existing customers include:

▶ Offer a discount on repeat orders that's exclusively for returning customers.

▶ Reward customers for every dollar they spend in your shop. For example, for every $100 they spend, they automatically receive a gift card worth $10 or $20.

▶ Encourage customers to sign up for (opt in to) a weekly, biweekly, or monthly email that will offer special discounts and promotions as well as useful information that the customer will find valuable. For example, you can share how-to information pertaining to your products, plus offer exclusive previews of new or soon-to-be released products.

▶ Publish a blog, and within it, promote special sales or discounts to existing customers.

▶ Create a birthday club that entitles existing customers to receive a special discount during their birthday month or within seven days of their birthday.

▶ Develop a referral promotion in which the existing customer receives a discount each time someone they refer places an order in your shop, and at the same time, that new customer receives a discount too for being a new (referred) customer.

▶ Interact and share information with your customers via your social media accounts, and promote online-only specials to your social media friends and followers.

▶ Provide your existing customers with the opportunity to purchase new items featured in your shop in advance of the general public.

▶ Create and distribute coupon codes to your existing customers (or potential customers) that offer a percentage discount off their next order, free shipping, or a savings of a fixed dollar amount. To learn how to create and utilize Etsy® Discount Codes, visit: www.Etsy.com/help/article/349.

Strategies for successfully using promotional emails, a blog, electronic newsletter, and/or social media to maintain communication with your existing customers are featured later in this chapter.

Rely on Your Positive Ratings and Reviews to Boost Your Credibility

Earning and then showcasing positive ratings and reviews from your past customers is a powerful tool for helping to convert visitors to your Etsy® shop into paying customers. As you'll quickly discover, positive ratings and reviews give your business instant credibility. These same reviews also allow your future customers to learn firsthand about the experiences of your past customers.

Your potential customers can quickly discover exactly what other people think about whatever it is you're selling. The ratings and reviews you receive are automatically and prominently displayed within your Etsy® shop. There's no way to hide them. That is why it is extremely important to put forth your best efforts to provide top-notch customer service, always be honest with your customers, sell only the highest quality products, fulfill and ship your orders promptly, and take steps to build strong relationships with your customers. After customers receive their order, it's then up to them to decide whether they want to write and publish a review about your product(s) and business. This is purely an optional activity on their part, but as you'll discover, it's a decision you can help influence.

As you'll discover shortly, there are simple steps you can take to encourage your customers to publish a positive review of your product(s), without you coming off as being pushy or unprofessional. Don't just sit back and hope your customers will help you out by posting a positive review. Most will not unless they're politely encouraged to do so.

Just as great reviews can help your business, earning poor ratings and reviews can literally destroy your business. Never underestimate the importance of Etsy®'s ratings and review system as you decide how you'll operate your business and ultimately treat your customers.

Chapter 7, "Always Offer Top-Notch Customer Service," explains how Etsy®'s Ratings and Review system works and provides advice for earning the best possible reviews.

Take Advantage of Etsy®'s Own SEO Tools

You already know that Etsy® has an established and loyal community comprised of members who enjoy browsing Etsy® and visiting various shops anytime they want or need to make a purchase. The easiest way to attract these potential customers to your shop is to take advantage of Etsy®'s SEO tools.

At the time you create your Etsy® shop, and then again when creating each product listing, you will be asked for keywords (tags) that clearly, accurately, and succinctly describe your business and products. Your objective is to include words that you believe your potential customers will use within Etsy®'s search field when looking for products that are similar to what you offer.

▶ Strategies for Compiling Your Keyword/Tag List

The best thing you can do to improve your Etsy® SEO search rankings is to provide a highly targeted, well-thought-out, accurate, and descriptive set of keywords/tags when describing your company and creating each of your product listings.

To help you come up with a list of popular tags/search words, visit Etsy® as a customer and start typing words or search phrases that describe what you're selling or your shop. As you type, the most popular and related search words or phrases will be displayed, in real time, directly below the search field. Consider using some of these suggestions when compiling your own keyword/tag list.

Remember that the wording within your product listing title is also searchable, so incorporate relevant keywords and tags there as well. Then make sure the category you select for the shop itself, as well as each item, is accurate and the most applicable.

Your keyword/tag list should include the following:

- ▶ Describe your item(s) in detail
- ▶ Who the items are for
- ▶ The material(s) used to create the item
- ▶ How the item is made
- ▶ How, where, and when the item can be used
- ▶ What size(s), color(s), and/or scent(s) the item comes in

As you're developing your keyword/tag list, consider synonyms that a shopper might use for the words/tags you've already come up with.

When the tags you include match a potential customer's search words, a listing for your shop or one of your product listings appears in that person's search results with a link directly to your shop or that product.

Etsy® determines your search result ranking based on a number of factors, which it does not fully disclose to sellers. These factors likely include how many search words/tags that the potential customer entered in the search field match the words/tags you provided, as well as how long you've been in business and your average ratings.

Ultimately, once you start generating traffic to your shop, Etsy® provides detailed analysis and information about those visitors. This information includes what keywords were used to find and visit your shop or product listings. Tracking this information is a fast and easy way to determine which of your keywords/tags is drawing the most traffic and which ones need to be fine-tuned or replaced with more commonly used words/tags.

aha!

Google provides a free, online tool for brainstorming keywords and tags. It was designed for people who use paid Google AdWords advertising to reach a highly targeted audience online, but you can use the same tool for coming up with keywords/tags for use on Etsy®. To find this tool, visit: https://adwords.google.com/KeywordPlanner.

Become Active on Social Media

On any given day, billions of computer and mobile device users around the world spend time on social media, such as Facebook, Twitter, Instagram, Pinterest, and YouTube. People tend to use social media for the following reasons:

- ▶ To stay in contact with their real-world friends and family
- ▶ To meet and interact with new people who share similar interests
- ▶ To display and share their photos
- ▶ To play online games with other people (on applicable services)
- ▶ To share their opinions on any topic(s) on their minds
- ▶ To participate in public special-interest groups, forums, or conversations related to specific topics
- ▶ To gather and learn new information
- ▶ To share their knowledge and expertise with others
- ▶ To interact with businesses
- ▶ As an alternative to watching TV, listening to the radio, or reading print media

More and more people are turning away from traditional media consumption habits, such as watching TV, listening to the radio, reading newspapers, and reading magazines. Instead, they are using social media to obtain whatever information they want or need in a format that's highly personalized and that's presented to them on an on-demand basis.

Social media has now become a place where business operators can freely and informally communicate with existing customers, seek out and draw in new customers, and establish an interactive online community that's based around their company and/or products.

As an Etsy® shop owner, it's not a matter of whether or not you should become active on social media. Without a doubt, you should! What you need to consider is, based on your target audience, your available time and resources, and what you're selling, which social media services will serve your needs the best.

Establish a Company and Personal Facebook Page

Many Etsy® shop owners have found success hosting a Facebook page for their business as well as a personal Facebook page. A company Facebook page can be branded with your logo, for example, and offers a free and easy way to establish an interactive online community comprised of anyone who is interested in your company or products.

The best way to get started is to establish a personal Facebook page first and populate it with basic information that you'd like to share about yourself, your business, and your work as an artist/artisan. Next, establish a Facebook page for your business that is linked to your personal Facebook page. To do this, visit www.Facebook.com from your computer and then click the Create a Page option from the drop-down menu next to the question mark in the upper-right corner of the screen.

Next, select the type of Facebook page you want to create. Related options include: Company, Organization or Institution; Brand or Product; or Cause or Community. Based on the descriptions provided by Facebook, choose the option that most applies. Then follow the on-screen prompts to populate your company Facebook page with content that you believe your potential and existing customers will find useful, informative, and entertaining. At the same time, encourage your Facebook audience to become active on your page by posting their own thoughts, opinions, reviews, and photos, for example.

Managing a Facebook page for your company is free but will require an ongoing investment of time. To make the page successful, you'll need to commit to publishing new content on a regular basis and to interacting with potential and existing customers who choose to participate in your virtual community.

There are many books, articles, and videos online about how to establish and operate a successful Facebook page for yourself and your business. Once your company's Facebook page is established, you can manage it on a day-to-day basis from your computer or by using the official Facebook Pages Manager mobile app that's available for iOS and Android smartphones and tablets.

What's great about a Facebook page is that it's highly customizable and it allows you to promote links to your Etsy® shop, company website, or other online-based activities. It can also be a place where you publish a blog or newsletter; share information that you believe your target audience will find useful; and showcase individual photos, photo galleries, or videos to your potential and existing customers. You can also solicit information and feedback from people and promote online-only sales. In fact, how you utilize Facebook as a powerful sales, marketing, and promotional tool is limited only by your own creativity and time investment.

Become Active on Twitter and/or Instagram

While Facebook allows participants to share unlimited information in a wide range of formats, Twitter and Instagram are a bit more structured and allow users to share small tidbits of information within a feed that is public and searchable.

Establishing a Twitter and/or Instagram account is free. You can create and manage an account from any internet-connected computer as well as any smartphone or tablet. Each post (or tweet) that you compose and publish in your Twitter feed (once you establish an account) can be up to 140 characters long, plus include a photo, video clip, and/or a website URL (such as a link to your Etsy® shop).

Instagram is very similar to Twitter; however, the emphasis is on sharing one image or video clip at a time with your audience. Each post can include a text caption as well as other information about the photo/video clip being posted, such as where it was taken and who appears within it. A website URL can also be included within the caption.

Twitter and Instagram are primarily public forums, which means that what you post can be found and seen by anyone. To help people easily find your tweets or Instagram postings, use hashtags (keywords preceded with the "#"), making your postings more easily searchable.

Anytime someone sees one of your tweets or Instagram posts, they can post a public comment, "like" the post or photo, or share it with their own followers and online friends. When people share your posts, this becomes a powerful tool for generating word-of-mouth publicity for your business or products.

Once again, many books, as well as free articles and how-to videos, are available to teach you how to properly and effectively use Twitter or Instagram as a powerful marketing, promotional, and sales tool. For example, Etsy® sellers often use one or both of these services to promote new products as well as online-only sales.

To get started using Twitter, visit www.twitter.com. To get started using Instagram, visit www.instagram. com or download the official Twitter or Instagram app for your mobile device. Keep in mind, both Twitter and Instagram now offer online and mobile app tools for managing a business Twitter or Instagram account, as well as to manage highly targeted, paid advertising campaigns on these services.

tip

What's great about Twitter and Instagram is that the learning curve to use them is very short. The available tools for reaching a highly targeted audience are powerful, and these services can be used to handle a variety of marketing tasks that can help build customer loyalty and drive traffic to your Etsy® shop.

Pinterest as a Viable Tool for Etsy® Sellers

Pinterest (www.pinterest.com) is another social media service that's particularly popular with crafters, artists, artisans, and other creative people because the service is primarily photo-based and encourages people to share and showcase their creative ideas.

Pinterest users can create and share photo, video, and text content in a way that can help Etsy® sellers establish and promote their brand, as well as their products.

To discover how to use Pinterest for business, visit: https://business.pinterest.com/en, or to begin setting up your own free account and exploring how this service works, visit www.pinterest.com from your computer or download and install the free Pinterest mobile app onto your smartphone or tablet. Many Etsy® sellers benefit from using Pinterest because it's a highly visual platform.

Operating a YouTube Channel Allows You to Share Your Videos

Many people think of YouTube as simply a place to watch free video content. However, it's become the number-two most popular internet search engine in the world. When web surfers want to find information about a topic, they enter what they're looking for into the YouTube search field and quickly discover dozens, perhaps hundreds, of entertaining, informative, and/or educational videos to watch for free on an unlimited and on-demand basis.

Companies that establish their own YouTube channel are able to group their videos into playlists and share them with the general public as well as their existing customers. In addition to sharing promotional videos designed to drive traffic to an online store, many Etsy® sellers use YouTube videos to offer in-depth video demonstrations of their products as well as video tutorials for putting together or using their products. Videos can also be used to tell a company's story, offer a "behind the scenes" look at a company and its products, and promote an individual as an expert in their field.

Yes, producing, editing, and publishing videos requires a lot more time and effort than managing a Twitter or Instagram account, for example, but presenting potential or existing customers with video content can be much more powerful.

To learn more about how to use YouTube to promote a business, pick up a copy of Entrepreneur Press's the *Ultimate Guide to YouTube for Business, Second Edition* by Jason R. Rich. You can also find information about YouTube by visiting these websites:

▶ YouTube Creator Hub: www.youtube.com/yt/creators
▶ YouTube Help: www.youtube.com/user/YouTubeHelp

tip

When done correctly, being active on social media allows you to reach a highly targeted audience that you define, and informally communicate with potential and existing customers. You can use social media to promote new products, offer how-to advice about your products, handle common customer service issues, encourage repeat business, offer online-only sales, and build a virtual (and loyal) community around your customers and product(s).

Use Email to Your Advantage

People hate receiving spam, which is unsolicited junk email that continuously appears in their inbox. However, when people want to receive information from a company or organization and they trust the potential sender, they're often willing to share their email address and voluntarily opt in to a company's email list.

Once a company compiles a list of the potential and existing customers that want to receive emails, it's possible to use email management software or an online service to compose and send personalized and targeted emails to these individuals on a consistent basis.

You can use personalized email messages to stay in touch with existing customers as well as entice potential customers to visit your Etsy® shop. Use email to promote online sales, showcase new products, answer commonly asked questions, provide valuable and informative information, and/or to distribute a company newsletter, for example.

To avoid the appearance of spam, your emails should be personalized, targeted to your audience, and include content that the recipients deem valuable and useful. Otherwise, they'll immediately disregard the incoming messages and unsubscribe from your email list.

Fee-based services, such as Boomerang (www. boomerang.com), Campaigner (www.campaigner. com), Constant Contact (www.constantcontact.com/ email-marketing), GetResponse (www.getresponse. com), and MailChimp (www.mailchimp.com) can help you establish, build, and manage your email marketing campaigns.

Consider Starting a Website, Blog, and/or Newsletter

In addition to operating your Etsy® shop, you have the ability to create, manage, and promote your own website, blog, and/or electronic newsletter. The benefit to having your own website, blog, or newsletter is that you have complete design and editorial control over the content. You can brand this content appropriately and then share it with your target audience.

If you discover that you're unable to tell your full story using the tools and resources currently available from Etsy®, consider creating your own website, blog, or newsletter using a separate service to create and share the your content however you deem most appropriate.

In addition to the time commitment required, creating and managing your own website typically costs money. You need to acquire your website domain name and then hire a website hosting service to host the site. Based on your technical skills, you may also need to hire a professional website designer to design the site itself and then populate it with your content.

warning

If you opt to use email as a marketing, sales, and promotional tool, make it very clear upfront how often members of your list will receive your messages and what the messages will typically include, and reassure them that their email address will not be sold or shared with other companies or organizations.

When you commit to a weekly, biweekly, or monthly email schedule, stick to it. Do not start harassing your recipients with daily emails or bombarding their inbox with too much information too frequently. This will cause them to unsubscribe from your mailing list and most likely turn them against your company.

Creating and managing a blog is a much easier and more cost-effective option than publishing a website. A blog can be created for free and then linked to your Etsy® shop and/or social media pages. You can make your blog/newsletter available to anyone or make it accessible to only invited guests or subscribers.

Blogging services you can use to create and manage a blog or newsletter include Blogger (www.blogger.com), WordPress (https://wordpress.org), Tumblr (www.tumblr.com), or Typepad (www.typepad.com). You can also use your company Facebook page to host a blog for free. Most of these services allow you to choose a theme-based template and then drag-and-drop or import your content into that template, so no programming or web design skill is required. Depending on the service you choose, there may be a learning curve involved as you get started.

tip

Companies such as GoDaddy, Wix, SiteBuilder, and eHost provide the tools and resources that non-tech-savvy people need to create and publish a website using online tools and templates, usually for an additional fee.

Plan and Execute a Public Relations Campaign

A public relations campaign should include specially formatted materials such as press releases about your company and products. These are designed to distribute to the media in hope that they will feature your information or a review of your product. Newspapers, magazines, blogs, radio programs, TV shows, or YouTube videos are all good outlets for this.

Depending on your objective, you may try to have yourself (or your key artist/artisan) get interviewed by media outlets. What's great about generating media publicity about your company is that it's free. However, creating and managing a public relations campaign does take time and effort, and it must be done correctly so that you're able to build strong relationships with editors, writers, reporters, bloggers, hosts, and YouTube personalities without harassing or alienating them.

Public relations (PR) can be mastered over time. However, you may find it easier to hire a freelance PR specialist, or a full-service firm that has experience, expertise, and established media contacts, to help you with this endeavor—especially if you're seeking national media exposure.

aha!

For free help creating and managing a blog, visit www.theblogstarter.com.

When creating a PR campaign, have realistic expectations, especially if you're a new business. First, have a

▶ Reach Out to Established Bloggers and YouTubers

One proven strategy for driving traffic to your Etsy® shop is to connect with established bloggers and YouTubers (online personalities who produce videos on YouTube) who review the type of product(s) you're selling and target the same niche audience as yours. Provide the blogger with a free product sample of what you offer as well as appropriate photos and press materials and then ask them to write about or review your products in their blog or videos.

Also determine if the blogger or YouTuber would be interested in featuring an interview with you or using you as a guest blogger/vlogger to supply content that you produce to their blog or YouTube channel.

Reaching out to bloggers is a grassroots and entry-level approach to public relations. It costs little to no money and can allow you to reach thousands, even millions, of potential customers. Be sure to focus your efforts by only contacting well-established bloggers who have large and loyal audiences.

To help you pinpoint the most influential bloggers that cater to the same target audience as your Etsy® shop, use one or more of these blog directories:

- ▶ Best of the Web Blogs search: https://blogs.botw.org
- ▶ Blog Catalog: www.blogcatalog.com
- ▶ Blog Search Engine: www.blogsearchengine.com
- ▶ Bloggapedia: www.bloggapedia.com
- ▶ BlogListing: www.bloglisting.net
- ▶ EatonWeb—The Blog Directory: http://portal.eatonweb.com
- ▶ OnToplist: www.ontoplist.com

Once you find the blogs you want, click on the About the Blogger or Contact options within the blog to find the blogger's name and email contact information. Many established bloggers will publish guidelines for submitting press materials and product samples for review.

Reaching out to bloggers as part of your public relations effort is a great way to build credibility for your business before you start approaching mainstream media for free publicity. However, when utilizing any type of public relations efforts, remember you do not have any control over what the blogger, reporter, reviewer, YouTuber, or journalist writes or says about your company or your products, and you do not control when you will be given the coverage you desire.

▶ **Reach Out to Established Bloggers and YouTubers,** continued

By providing the media (including bloggers and YouTubers) with well-written press materials, you are able to communicate your marketing message in a stylized way that adheres to your brand. How the recipient utilizes the information you provide when writing/producing their article, review, or video, however, is out of your hands.

compelling and attention-getting story to tell, and then focus on targeting local or niche-oriented media first. Don't expect that you'll immediately be able to get booked as a guest of *The Today Show*, for example.

The easiest way to start building your public relations skills, and at the same time, generate some free publicity for your business or products, is to create a small, grass-roots effort that targets influential bloggers and YouTubers (online personalities).

When approaching media people, at the very least you need to supply a well-written and properly formatted press release. You can also include a company background information sheet and written bios of your company executives and/or key artists/artisans.

Then create a highly targeted media list that's comprised of editors, writers, reporters, bloggers, hosts, and YouTube personalities who specifically cover topics related to your company or products. For example, if you're a jewelry maker, you don't want to send your press release to the financial, sports, or national news editors at a publication. Instead, you probably want to target the fashion editor or small-business editor.

To find the appropriate people to contact, you can purchase a targeted media list from companies such as Cision (www.cision.com) or work with a fee-based press release distribution service such as PR Newswire (www.prnewswire.com), SocialMediaWire (http://socialmediawire.net), PRWeb (www.prweb.com), or eReleases (www.ereleases.com).

For information on how to write and format a proper press release, use any internet search engine and enter "How to write a press release" in the search field. You'll find dozens of detailed how-to articles that describe how to do this from services such as wikiHow (www.wikihow.com/Write-a-Press-Release) and Huffington Post (www.huffingtonpost.com/zach-cutler/press-release-tips_b_2120630.html).

To find a freelance publicist you can hire, use a service such asUpwork (www.upwork.com), Freelancer (www.freelancer.com), Simply Hired (www.simplyhired.com), or LinkedIn (www.linkedin.com).

If you have the budget, you can find a local, full-service public relations firm by performing an online search, obtaining a referral from someone you know, or by accessing an online PR firm directory such as the Public Relations Society of America (www.prsa. org/Network/FindAFirm/Search), O'Dwyer's (www.odwyerpr.com/pr_firms_database/ index.htm), or PRChannel (www.prchannel.com).

Take Part in Local and Regional Craft Fairs

Yet another way to drive traffic to your Etsy® store is to display and sell your work at local or regional craft fairs throughout the year. In addition to providing potential customers with the opportunity to meet you and see your work firsthand, you can promote your Etsy® store by giving away promotional items such as business cards, printed fliers, catalogs, or postcards that have your Etsy® shop's website address clearly displayed.

Paid Advertising Typically Offers Faster Results, But at a Financial Cost

If you're willing to invest some money to drive traffic to your Etsy® store using paid advertising, you have a wide range of opportunities. You'll typically achieve the best and quickest results if you focus on paid advertising on social media, paid advertising on search engines, and/or paid advertising on Etsy® itself.

When you use paid online advertising, you determine the exact message you want to convey, have the ability to carefully target your audience, and can often choose a "pay-per-click" method that only requires you to pay a fee when someone actually visits your website or Etsy® store. You also decide when and where someone will see your message.

The startup costs to create and launch an online ad campaign is typically between $50 and $100, although you can set whatever budget you want. If you use the advertising tools correctly, the more you spend, the more traffic you'll drive to your shop.

Some of the key advantages of paid online advertising include:

- ▶ You have 100 percent control over the ad message.
- ▶ You decide when and where someone sees your ad.
- ▶ You're able to reach a highly targeted audience that you define.
- ▶ The startup costs for a campaign are very low (compared to advertising with traditional media).
- ▶ You can create and launch a new campaign typically within a few hours and start seeing results almost immediately.
- ▶ You can tweak or fine-tune a campaign as it's running to enhance its effectiveness.

▶ You're able to track the success of your campaign in real time and determine what's working (and quickly fix what's not working).

To get started with an online ad campaign, first determine where you want your ads to appear. Some of the most popular options include:

▶ Bing Ads: https://advertise.bingads.microsoft.com

▶ Facebook Advertising: www.facebook.com/business

▶ Google AdWords: https://adwords.google.com

▶ Instagram Advertising: https://business.instagram.com/advertising

▶ Twitter Advertising: https://ads.twitter.com

▶ Yahoo! Advertising: https://advertising.yahoo.com

Before you invest money pursuing any of these online advertising opportunities, make sure you understand exactly how each service works and what fees apply. Then use the available tools and resources provided by that service to create the best ad possible so that it targets your intended audience and conveys the most precise, attention-getting, and accurate message possible. In some cases, a product photo or company logo can be displayed with your text-based ad message. This is useful if you're trying to sell specific products, for example.

Use Etsy® Advertising to Promote Your Etsy® Shop

In addition to using Etsy®'s SEO tools to help drive traffic to your shop, another option is to take advantage of Etsy®'s paid advertising opportunities that will allow your shop or selected product listings to be prominently featured. When you pay Etsy® to promote your product listings, this is called a Promoted Listing.

Etsy® uses an auction-based process for determining the placement of your paid Promoted Listing because it's likely that several companies offering products similar to yours are also using Promoted Listing to drive traffic to their shops.

According to Etsy®, two main factors are used for determining Promoted Listing ad placement. First, there's

warning

Make sure whatever you're selling on Etsy® is profitable enough for you to justify the cost of Promoted Listings. If you wind up paying more per click than you make in profit from each sale, this type of advertising is not best suited to meet your needs. Also, assuming your campaign generates positive results, make sure you have the inventory on hand to quickly fill the new orders you receive and that you have the time in your schedule to fill those orders promptly.

how much you're willing to pay for each click to your shop. This is called your bid. Second, based on the content in your listing, the history of your shop, and the way you've utilized tags and keywords, Etsy® determines how likely it is that someone who views your listing will click on the displayed link. This is referred to as the linking quality.

tip

To learn more about Promoted Listings and how they can benefit you, visit: www.Etsy.com/help/article/49190700688. To start using Etsy® Advertising, visit: www.Etsy.com/advertising.

Your bid is the highest amount you're willing to pay per click. The more you're willing to bid, the better your listing placement will be in each buyer's search results when someone uses the Etsy® Search tool to find what they're looking for.

Because Etsy® constantly reevaluates each Promoted Listing, its placement in search results will often change, sometimes several times within a several-hour period. The benefit to Etsy® advertising is that your product listing(s) receive increased visibility in Etsy®'s buyer community that uses Etsy®'s search tool. It's also possible to create and launch a campaign in minutes and then gain insight into your customers by studying the results of your campaigns.

Once you opt to launch an Etsy® Promoted Listing campaign, you'll be asked to set your Maximum Daily Budget for the campaign. The minimum is $1.00 per day. This service is constantly evolving, so check the Etsy® website for the latest information on how to set up and manage a campaign.

Then, as you're managing the campaign, make sure you understand the difference between the impressions (views) your Promoted Listing receives versus the number of clicks it receives. You can also track how much you're paying per click versus how much revenue you generate per click (assuming someone makes a purchase after seeing your listing). All this information, and more, can be tracked in real time.

As you're evaluating a campaign's results, you may find it beneficial to update a product listing by choosing more appropriate keywords/tags, altering the title, or providing more detail within the description, for example.

Determine If Advertising in Special Interest Publications Can Be Beneficial

Many of the most successful Etsy® sellers know their target audience(s) for their products and figure out the very best ways to reach this audience—both in the real world and online.

Thus, you may find it useful to use paid advertising in special interest or niche publications that reach the exact audience you're trying to promote to.

These publications may be printed magazines or newsletters, or they could be online forums, users' groups, special interest groups, blogs, or other types of websites. Once you figure out which publications or media outlets are targeting the same audience you want to reach, contact each outlet to determine its advertising rates and policies. Then determine if creating and running a paid ad campaign with that media outlet is economically viable.

Keep in mind that with most forms of traditional advertising, it will be necessary for you to achieve multiple impressions from your potential leads before they respond to the ad or click on the provided link. Thus, you may wind up needing to run your ad over the course of several days, weeks, or months before you start generating a response.

Based on the response you receive, you can easily calculate your cost per response (or cost per click) and then determine whether it's more cost effective to continue with that media outlet or seek out other advertising opportunities that allow you to reach more people at a lower cost.

Determine Your Advertising and Marketing Budget

After researching the paid advertising opportunities that are available to you, figure out how much money you have available to spend on advertising on a daily, weekly, or monthly basis. Determine if the money for each ad campaign is coming directly out of your profit from sales or if in addition to the amount of each sale you've allocated to be profit, you've also added an advertising expense when calculating and determining the pricing for whatever you'll be selling.

Then, once you begin experimenting with each advertising opportunity, track the results carefully. Make sure the profit you're earning from the additional sales at the very least covers the cost of the ads you're running. Based on the results of each campaign, determine whether you can achieve better results by tweaking the campaign or whether you've selected the wrong advertising opportunities altogether.

Expect a learning curve as you research the ins and outs of advertising. Consider hiring someone with advertising experience to help you, at least initially, to ensure you make the most cost-effective decisions as you create and implement each new campaign.

Advertising can work very well for you as an Etsy® seller, but you need to use it properly. Make sure you develop the right message, target the right audience, and use the right tools available to you from each advertising opportunity to track and then fine-tune your results as needed.

Meet Jewelry Maker Luann Udell

Luann Udell (www.Etsy.com/shop/LuannUdell) has been an artist for more than two decades. When she decided to begin selling her work online, she selected Etsy® as the service she'd use to host her store. "My work is really unusual, it's expensive, and it's handmade. Using primarily polymer clay, I make these artifacts that look like prehistoric carvings. The work is inspired by pieces that are between 15,000 and 30,000 years old," she explains. "These artifacts look authentic. The small ones are worn as jewelry, and the larger pieces are displayed as sculptures."

Udell explains that she has wanted to be an artist since she was a child. However, it wasn't until her children were grown up that she decided to pursue being an artist professionally. She was in her mid-40s at the time. "There was one point in my life when I just realized that I needed to become a full-time artist, or I would die," she recalls. "I discovered an art history book that focused on the Lascaux Cave in France, and that really inspired me and my work. I am inspired by a lot of ancient cultures."

As soon as Udell began selling her work online, she quickly discovered that it was necessary to acquire some core business skills which she did not already possess. "I also needed to discover how to write a powerful artist statement and learn how to properly talk about and describe my work so other people could connect to it. This has been a wonderful journey for me so far," says Udell, who also maintains a blog about her work and her journey as an artist (https://luannudell.wordpress.com).

"Etsy® caters primarily to the handmade market and has a very dedicated and large audience of customers. It's a user-friendly service, and a lot of people enjoy shopping on it. I view my presence on Etsy® as a standalone shop for my collectors and my prospective collectors. I don't necessarily try to target the mainstream Etsy® audience," says Udell, "although I do draw customers who were simply exploring the Etsy® service." Figure 6–1 on page 136 shows Udell's shop on Etsy®.

Beyond selling on Etsy®, Udell has tried using other online services to showcase and sell her work. She's also participated in high-end craft shows around the country and has sold her work through galleries. Ultimately, however, much of her success selling her work has been a result of her presence on Etsy®. "So many people think that they can craft something, put it online, and it will be an instant success selling on Etsy®. This is just not the case. The reality is that very few, if any, people on Etsy® become an overnight success. It takes time to build an audience and a reputation, no matter what you're selling," says Udell.

"When I started selling on Etsy®, I knew it would take time to establish myself, and I also knew that my work was not for everyone and that it caters to a niche audience. I

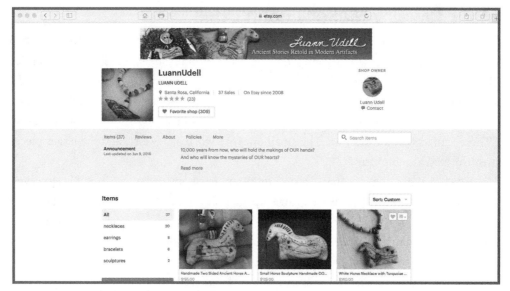

FIGURE 6-1: **Luann Udell's Etsy® Shop**

think the biggest mistake first-time Etsy® sellers make is not giving their store the time to be successful. After a few days or weeks with no sales, they think they're doing something wrong or that their work isn't good enough. This is typically not the case. You just need to be patient and persistent and not expect instant success," explains Udell.

When asked what components she believes go into a perfect store on Etsy®, Udell responded, "It's important to have a consistent message throughout your store and showcase a cohesive body of work. It's also essential that you put in the time to discover who your core customers or collectors are and learn how to properly target those people using the content in your store, as well as through your marketing efforts. Another strategy that will help a seller achieve success is that they should continuously update their store with new products, photos, and content. Don't just create the online store and leave it stagnant for weeks or months at a time. If you post listings for items and then sell out of those items be sure to update your store promptly and accordingly."

Currently, Udell considers her Etsy® business to be a serious hobby that allows her to earn a part-time income. "I earn enough money to contribute to my household, but I don't make enough money yet to support myself financially. That being said, I didn't start doing this with the goal of getting wealthy. I do this because it is a passion. I don't have to be financially successful doing this. If I needed to support myself completely from this, I would certainly do things a bit differently," she says.

Having run her Etsy® store for several years now, from a financial standpoint, her biggest financial investment has been in having high-quality product images taken by a professional photographer.

"My biggest expense has always been obtaining high-quality images of my work. I tried to take my own images, but they turned out awful. I wound up finding a photographer who lives 30 minutes away from me and who offers discounted rates to other artists and artisans. He turned out to be a talented photographer who worked quickly and who was affordable. All of the advertising and marketing I have done to promote my store and my work, and the appearance of the store itself, is all based around my product photos," says Udell, who believes that too many sellers on Etsy® don't really understand how important it is to have really good product images.

"When you're selling anything online, people can't touch and experience your work firsthand. Your images represent you and your work. They need to be crystal clear, in focus, visually appealing, attention-getting, and truly showcase what you're selling in the best way possible. I am shocked when I browse Etsy® and I see so many poor-quality photos. My suggestion is that if you don't have the ability to take your own professional-quality product photos, you should develop an ongoing relationship with a photographer," adds Udell.

Udell discovered firsthand that product photography is a skill and art form in itself. Even if you hire a professional photographer, it needs to be someone with experience doing product photography and who understands your work. Ultimately, when the photographer she was using passed away, she developed the skill necessary to take her own product shots.

"I have friends who sell their work on Etsy® and who take their own good-quality product shots using the camera that's built into their smartphone. This approach is certainly possible, and it works fine for some types of products, assuming your shots properly utilize lighting, are in focus, and adequately showcase what you are selling. If you are able to develop the skill necessary to take your own photos, it makes the process of continuously updating, expanding, and maintaining your store so much easier," she explains.

As for the backgrounds Udell uses in her product shots, she tends to be creative. "There is an old, painted wooden box that I purchased at a flea market I often use as a background in my product shots, as opposed to a solid white background. After I take my product shots, I edit them using the photo editing software that come preinstalled on my computer. It's so easy. I don't understand how any Etsy® seller would even consider not having good product photos when they have so many options for being able to use really great photos in their store," says Udell.

One of Udell's early mistakes when she first created her Etsy® store was that she set it up, populated it with a few items to sell, and then allowed it to sit dormant and unchanged for several months at a time while orders slowly trickled in. She now updates the content in her store regularly.

She adds, "I think sellers also need to understand the mentality of buyers in today's online marketplace. People don't want to wait days or weeks after placing an order to receive it. If they go online and find what they want to purchase, they expect to receive that order very quickly. If the item is out of stock or delayed for whatever reason, the customer will simply do another online search to find a similar item and then buy it elsewhere. Sellers need to be extremely attentive to their buyers and fill their orders promptly."

Beyond responding to inquiries from potential collectors quickly and then filling and shipping orders the same day they're received, Udell now relies on social media to promote her work and her online store.

"Many of my collectors follow me on Facebook, Instagram, or Twitter, for example. Each time I create a new piece, I post of photo of it on each of my social media accounts. This generates a lot of excitement and chatter about each new piece, and it offers a preview of what will soon be sold in my Etsy® store," says Udell. "This approach does a lot for generating repeat business from my collectors. I think it's important to promote yourself on multiple social media platforms simultaneously to build a strong connection with your customers."

Udell also attributes her success on Etsy® to the reputation she's built online. Having positive, five-star ratings and reviews boosts her online credibility with new customers, which she believes is very important when selling higher-priced items.

"Another important factor that many first-time sellers don't initially consider is how they'll ship orders to their customers in a cost-effective way. Sellers need to offer fast shipping options that include the ability to track and insure packages.

"It's important to determine the type of box and the shipping materials you'll need to safely ship your items, and then choose the best shipping options that will allow your items to arrive quickly and safely at their destination," says Udell, who really appreciates the latest tool Etsy® has added for sellers—the ability to offer multiple shipping options to customers.

When it comes to setting her prices, Udell does not pay attention to what her competition is selling similar items for. Instead, she calculates her prices based on the time she invests creating each product, the material costs, and how easy it is for her to acquire the materials for each piece. "I use a lot of antique and collectible beads, as well as semiprecious stones and pearls in my work, for example. Over time, I have gradually raised my prices as my work has become more refined, better known, and in greater demand," adds Udell. "How every Etsy® seller sets their prices is a personal decision. I don't think there is a set formula that everyone can follow."

Looking back, Udell believes that learning the photography skills needed to take great product shots was the hardest skill she needed to develop in regard to establishing and managing her Etsy® store.

She explains, "I also had to learn all about social media. Most recently, I taught myself how to use Instagram, which was not as difficult as I thought it would be. Today, using social media to communicate with customers or collectors is essential. Instagram in particular is very useful for artists because it's photo based and it's easier to use than Pinterest. Instagram can be used to showcase your own work and give you access to people who are otherwise completely unknown to you. I am also active on Facebook and Twitter."

As an artist, Udell also needed to learn how to talk about and describe her work. She adds, "I am a talker. I also love to tell stories. However, as an artist, I always thought that art has to speak for itself. This is not necessarily the case. In many situations, it's up to the artist to be able to explain their work in an attention-getting, interesting, but not arrogant way. People want to know the story behind a work of art.

"People selling on Etsy® need to understand how to communicate with prospective customers, as well as their existing customers. They also need to provide top-notch customer service before and after a sale has been made.

"I provide really good customer care, even when I know the customer is wrong. Sometimes you can't offer adequate customer service using email. Sometimes a phone call with your customer is necessary to understand what the customer's issue really is and reach a solution to the problem that both parties are comfortable with. Only once have I needed to tell a customer to return their purchase in exchange for a refund."

The biggest tip Udell offers to new Etsy® sellers is to focus on the essence of whatever it is you're doing and figure out how to best communicate that to showcase your work on the Etsy® platform within your store.

"Etsy® has made creating an online store almost foolproof, even if you're not tech-savvy. What a seller needs to do using the tools available to them is to tell their own unique story in an interesting and compelling way. Sellers need to use their store to tell people why they should give a crap about whatever it is you're selling. It's the unique story that you're able to tell that will set whatever it is you're selling apart from the competition," says Udell.

She concludes, "Based on my experience, I have found that Etsy® is accessible, easy to use, has an excellent reputation, and it's well-known. Etsy® makes it very easy for people who want to find and buy my work to make an online purchase. In a nutshell, I can't sing Etsy®'s praises high enough. In my opinion, the other services that allow artists to sell their work online are all trying to be Etsy®."

Additional Thoughts

Once you establish your business, it's essential that you adopt a multifaceted approach to promoting it and that you take steps to continuously drive a steady flow of traffic to your Etsy® shop and/or other online platforms. These marketing, promotional, and advertising tasks will ultimately require your ongoing attention and can't be skipped.

Unfortunately, simply establishing the shop is not enough. If you don't promote it on an ongoing basis, you won't get customers. Without customers, you won't have sales. Without sales, there's no money to be earned. Then, assuming you do everything correctly, drive a steady flow of traffic to your shop, and transform visitors to your shop into paying customers, you then must focus on making every customer's shopping experience the best it can possibly be. Creating and implementing top-notch customer service efforts is the focus of the next chapter.

Always Offer Top-Notch Customer Service

All the interaction you have with your prospective and current customers becomes part of their overall customer service experience. It's your job as the Etsy® seller and business operator to make that experience as favorable as possible. However, even if you go out of your way to make your customers happy, there will always be situations when something goes wrong and someone winds up disgruntled.

When (not if) this happens, your primary task must be to turn the situation around and transform the unhappy customer into a happy one. To do this, you must first determine exactly why that person is upset and discover directly from them what will make it better. Listen to your customer. Then you must decide whether you're willing to take those steps.

Ways to Handle Customer Service

If you live by that saying, "The customer is always right," then you will need to take whatever actions are necessary to remedy the situation, regardless of whether or not you agree with the customer. In some cases, this might mean you will need to forego your profit on that sale or even lose some money to keep that customer happy.

Allowing a customer to remain unhappy leads to problems and can easily tarnish your reputation as a seller. For example, disappointed customers can react adversely in the following ways:

tip

Providing the best possible customer service will help you enhance your brand. By going beyond what's expected by your shop's visitors and customers, and continuously exceeding their expectations, you will be taking a major step toward developing and maintaining what people will perceive as a premium brand. If your customers perceive you're giving them greater value for the money they're spending, they'll be more apt to pay higher prices, plus feel really good about their purchases and their shopping experience.

- ▶ Write and publish a negative rating and review on Etsy® (which permanently becomes accessible to other people)
- ▶ Share their negative experience about your company and/or products with their friends, family, and coworkers, encouraging them never to support your business
- ▶ Post negative comments about you on social media, which remains online indefinitely and could potentially be read by dozens, hundreds, or thousands of people
- ▶ Never become a repeat customer
- ▶ Demand a full refund for whatever it is they've purchased including shipping and handling fees to and from the customer
- ▶ File a negative report about your business with the Better Business Bureau
- ▶ Report your business to PayPal, Apple Pay, or their credit card company
- ▶ Cost you a lot of time, money, and aggravation

On the other hand, if you do what's necessary to provide top-notch service to all your prospective and current customers, make it clear that they are extremely important to you. Take steps to make them feel welcome and special when they're shopping, and a wide range of extremely positive things will likely happen, for example:

▶ Help you increase your conversion rate among the people visiting your shop and transform more of them into paying customers

▶ If you offer multiple products, help encourage customers to increase or expand their initial order before they check out

▶ Encourage your existing customers to return to your shop often and become repeat customers

▶ Increase your chances of receiving a positive rating and review that gets published on Etsy®

▶ Increase your chances of receiving positive word-of-mouth promotion from your customers (both in person and online), which will lead to more customers and greater demand for your products, plus help boost your reputation and credibility

▶ Make running your Etsy® shop and interacting with your customers more enjoyable and less stressful

▶ Assist you in positively differentiating your business from your competition

▶ Increase the perceived value of your products, making customers feel more comfortable about their purchases

▶ Help you maximize your profits and reduce your financial losses

As you can see, making sure that you always offer superior customer service provides a win-win situation for you, your potential customers, and all your paying customers.

> **warning**
>
> In general, the Etsy® community is comprised of nice people. However, one of the biggest mistakes you can make as a seller is to allow yourself to argue with a customer, discriminate against a customer, or disrespect someone in any way. Even if someone yells at or verbally abuses you, don't drop to that level. Remain professional and polite. You always have the option to refuse a sale or return someone's money and walk away. If you do this, be polite about it.

Good Customer Service Requires More Than Just Saying "Thank You"

Every aspect of a visitor's experience at your shop and their interaction with you should be well thought-out and designed so that the customer feels welcome and special. You must make every customer genuinely believe that you (the seller) understand and respect their wants and needs. This means respecting their time, charging them fair prices, and making their shopping experience as stress-free and enjoyable as possible.

Providing the best possible customer service requires three main skills:

1. Good verbal and written communication skills
2. The ability to focus on and pay attention to detail
3. Keeping yourself well-organized so you're able to address and handle problems whenever they arise as quickly and efficiently as possible

21 Strategies for Providing Top-Notch Customer Service

The following are 21 strategies an Etsy® seller should implement on an ongoing basis to provide the best possible customer service:

1. Make yourself as accessible as possible. Display your email address and phone number prominently and repeatedly in your shop, and make it clear that questions are welcome. Then respond to inquiries as quickly as possible (within minutes or hours, not within days), especially if they're received during normal business hours. When you do receive a question, or list of questions, make sure you address each question with a complete and kind answer (even if you believe the question is stupid), and personalize the communication.

2. Do your best to make each customer feel important and special. When communicating with them one on one, make them feel as if they have your complete and undivided attention.

3. Fulfill and ship new orders as quickly as possible and always within the time frame that you've promised.

tip

Reminisce about your own experiences as a consumer shopping on Etsy®, being a customer with other online merchants, and shopping in the real world. As a customer, what shopping experiences stick out in your mind as being pleasurable, easy, and stress-free? What was it about those experiences that made them stand out? Now that you're a business operator, try to replicate those same experiences and feelings for your own customers.

At the same time, think about negative shopping experiences you've had. Define what made them awful, and then take steps as a shop owner to avoid those pitfalls. Learn from your own experiences as a shopper, and apply them as a seller.

4. Make sure that all the content in your shop is written or presented in an upbeat, accurate, and professional style that caters to your target audience. All the information you present, especially in your product descriptions, should be accurate and complete.

5. Anticipate your customers' questions, concerns, and needs, and present easy-to-understand answers and solutions in the Shipping and Shop Policies and/or FAQ section of your shop, for example, as well as in your product listings.

6. Always maintain a professional demeanor in all communication with your shop's visitors and customers, especially when the other person is upset and acts irrationally.

7. Check your work and avoid mistakes. Make sure that your products are free of defects and are high quality and that all orders are filled correctly and adhere to the customer's requests.

8. Once a customer places an order, stay in touch with them via email, letting them know the status of their order, the shipping details, and exactly when they can expect to receive their order.

9. Make it clear that your customers are important to you, and be grateful for their support. You can easily convey this is in the "About" section of your shop as you tell your story, as well as in your profile. You can also show your appreciation by including a thank-you message when someone places an order and a short but personalized handwritten message within the package when shipping your product(s).

10. Promote your refund policy, exchange policy, money-back guarantee, shipping policies, warranties, and any other important details that your customers need to know. This information should be displayed prominently and clearly. Be willing, however, to make exceptions in your customer's favor when special circumstances arise. Be understanding and flexible.

11. Within the shop itself, use the phrase "Thank you" repeatedly, including on the welcome page and when confirming a new order.

12. Make your shop easy to navigate and keep it uncluttered. If you offer many products, organize them into well-labeled sections.

13. Promote the fact that you welcome everyone's thoughts, feedback, and suggestions, even if

aha!

If a language barrier exists between you and your customer, consider using an online translator when necessary, such as Google Translator (https://translate.google.com) to ensure reliable and accurate communication.

they're not paying customers. If someone issues a complaint, thank them for bringing the matter to your attention and vow to address the situation immediately.

14. Beyond your Etsy® shop, offer free content to your followers on social media that the people in your target audience will find informative, entertaining, and valuable. Encourage ongoing, informal communication through social media (Facebook, Twitter, Instagram, Pinterest, YouTube, etc.).

15. Never harass a customer or prospective customer. If they opt into your email list, for example, use this communication sparingly, no more than once per week. Instead, encourage more frequent and informal communication through social media.

16. When a problem arises, address it immediately and do what's necessary to make the customer happy so they don't turn against you by posting a negative rating and review or publishing negative information via social media, for example.

17. If a package gets lost, damaged, or stolen after you've shipped it, take responsibility. Track the package and talk to the shipper promptly so you can explain to the customer what happened and immediately send them a replacement. Then file the insurance claim with the shipper as needed. It's your responsibility to deal with the shipper.

18. If you make a mistake, promptly apologize and go out of your way to fix the mistake. This might mean offering a partial or full refund, free shipping, an extra item in the customer's order, and/or a big discount on a subsequent order. Acknowledge the mistake and take responsibility for it.

19. Assuming you're proud and excited about operating your own business and believe it's a privilege to be doing so, make this clear as you interact with visitors and customers.

20. When you package your products for shipping to each customer, create a positive experience for them as they open that package. In addition to a personalized

tip

Your customer service actions will play a huge role in the ratings and reviews you receive, as well as increase or decrease your chances of receiving repeat business from a customer. Even if the customer only needs one of the items you're selling, if they love their purchase and enjoy their shopping experience, they may become a repeat customer so they can give your item(s) away as gifts in the future. Always try to build a long-term and ongoing relationship with each and every customer.

(preferably handwritten) thank-you note, try to emulate the process of opening a gift to enhance the receiver's experience. Consider using ribbons and tissue paper, for example, and focus on what the customer will see and feel as they open your package.

21. If you have a question for your customer about their order, obtain the answer before you proceed. Don't guess. Take the time to contact the customer via email or telephone and ask them to clarify whatever is unclear or to provide whatever information they forgot to include with their order (such as a color or size choice, a proper shipping address, or directions you need to create a custom order).

tip

Remember, customer service requires clear, concise, and ongoing communication that maintains a professional demeanor, regardless of the circumstances. If a problem or concern arises, address it and stick with it until a viable solution that's acceptable to your customer is achieved. Never drop the ball and allow a situation to accidentally get dropped or ignored, and if you make a promise or commitment to a customer, keep it.

Starting the moment you begin creating your shop and developing the content for it, focus on every step of the experience that your visitors will have, and do whatever possible to enhance it. Be sure to cater specifically to your target audience. What they see, how content is presented, the accessibility of information, and the clarity with which you communicate are all important. Just as important is your own attitude and how you make people feel when they communicate with you via email or telephone.

Every person who visits your shop will have expectations. It's important that their overall experience always meet or exceed those expectations, with no exceptions. By clearly defining your target audience and developing a true understanding of who these people are, you'll develop a much better understanding of their expectations, allowing you to anticipate their wants, needs, and concerns so you can address them promptly.

Meet Michelle Bold, Proprietor of Paintspiration

Paintspiration (www.Etsy.com/shop/Paintspiration) is Michelle Bold's Etsy® store from which she sells inspirational, motivational, and feel-good artwork and related products that she refers to as "art with a message." She also operates a second Etsy® store, called MiniZenGarden (www.Etsy.com/shop/MiniZenGarden), from which Bold sells small

Zen gardens and yoga-inspired items. Figures 7–1 and 7–2 show Michelle Bold's two Etsy® shops.

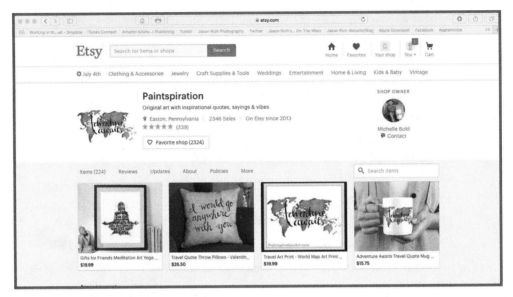

FIGURE 7–1: **Bold's Paintspiration Shop on Etsy®**

FIGURE 7–2: **Bold's Mini Zen Garden Shop on Etsy®**

"I create unique art through painting and on my computer that incorporates inspirational quotes and artwork," she explains. "I sell the designs on canvas and in print form but also have partnered with a company that imprints my art onto mugs, throw pillows, smartphone cases, and a wide range of other products. Before I started this Etsy® business, I was working as a mental health therapist in Washington, DC. My fiancé and I decided to move to North Carolina. I found a counselling job there and had everything set up, but once we made the move, the job fell through. I was having trouble finding a traditional job, so I decided to start the first Etsy® shop to sell my paintings. This was in early 2013."

Bold is a self-taught artist who enjoys creating paintings with inspirational messages. "I initially made gifts for friends and family, and several people suggested that I start selling my work on Etsy®. My work now blends my artistic talents and creativity with my counselling background. Lately, some of my work has also incorporated a travel theme because I really love to travel. I also do yoga-inspired artwork and sell desktop Zen gardens from my second Etsy® shop. These are little sand boxes with mini rakes that you comb in order to relax," she explains.

The reason why she divided her work into two separate shops is because she wanted each shop to have a unique but cohesive look that featured related products. The Zen gardens did not fit nicely into a shop that was selling artwork with inspirational quotes.

"I chose Etsy® because it's very user-friendly, and it's much easier to set up an Etsy® shop than it is to set up your own ecommerce website. Once you set up your shop, Etsy® takes care of your payment processing, for example. Etsy® also has a lot of its own traffic, which helps to drive customers to your store. Another thing I really like about Etsy® is the very low startup cost and the low ongoing fees the service charges for product listings, for example.

"If you're trying to sell art from your own website, you have to drive 100 percent of the traffic to that site. With Etsy®, potential customers who browse the service can stumble on your store based on keyword searches, for example," says Bold.

"Initially, I fell into the trap as a new Etsy® seller where I just assumed my target market consisted of absolutely everyone. I quickly learned, however, that when selling online, it's very important to narrow down your target market and then find ways to reach that niche audience. For example, for my travel-inspired art, I target people who enjoy travel. For my yoga-inspired art, I target people who practice yoga. This targeting applies to the design and content I offer within my Etsy® store but also to all online advertising and marketing that I do," she says.

Bold had a good friend who was successful selling handmade jewelry through her own Etsy® store prior to Bold starting her own store. "I had seen Etsy® work for her and was inspired by her success. I also had someone I could go to for guidance early on as I was setting up my own store. Initially, I did not have high hopes for what would happen with my first Etsy® store in terms of its success, but it quickly exceeded my expectations on many levels," explains Bold, who now operates her two Etsy® stores as her full-time job, although she also sells her work through other online services and venues.

She recalls that it initially took her three months of putting in long hours to really establish her first Etsy® store and begin generating enough revenue to pay her living expenses. "After the Etsy® shop was established, my now-husband and I decided to take off and travel the world for two years, and during that time I operated the business remotely and it was my sole source of income. I was able to do this by transferring a lot of my work into digital downloads, which I sold through Etsy®. I also used third-party vendors to create and ship the products that featured my artwork and designs. These products were created and shipped on an on-demand basis. This made it very easy to manage my store from overseas," says Bold.

Before she selected a third-party manufacturer to create and drop-ship her products on an on-demand basis, she did a lot of research to choose which company to work with. "I needed to make sure their product quality was good, that they offered good customer service, and that they were reliable. After all, I had to relinquish a lot of control and responsibility to this company that would ultimately be creating my products and shipping them directly to my customers. This was the biggest decision I had to make. I made a master list of companies that printed art on demand and then weeded one out at a time based on a wide range of criteria. Ultimately, I selected a company called Fine Art America (www.fineartamerica.com) to work with.

"Once I returned to the United States and was able to operate my company from home, I found a different printer and began doing my own shipping, for example, in order to lower my costs and regain more control over my business. I still use Fine Art America for some products, however, and they are a great company to work with," says Bold.

Looking back to when she started her Etsy® store, one thing Bold would have done differently was put more focus on SEO when creating her product listings, company name, and company description, and when adding other content to her Etsy® store.

She explains, "Etsy® encourages you to add keywords and descriptions to your store and product listings, which are used to help your store and products show up in keyword searches. I didn't pay too much attention to this initially, which made it harder for people to find my online store. Another thing I quickly discovered I needed to improve was the quality of my product photos. At first, they looked very amateurish. I do all my own product photography, but I needed to learn about using indirect natural light when taking product photos. I also had to learn how to use digital mockups as a way to showcase my artwork online. Ultimately, I invested in a higher-quality digital camera, spent time learning how to use it, and learned how to incorporate good lighting into my product shots. I also had to become proficient using photo editing software."

Now that her Etsy® stores have become successful, Bold believes that focusing on SEO when creating content for the Etsy® store is essential. "I generate most of my business as a result of people doing a keyword search with Etsy®'s Search tool. If you don't properly use the SEO tools that Etsy® offers, no matter how good your products are, they are not going to be seen. Then, once a potential customer reaches my store, I believe it's important to offer a professional and visually appealing appearance that caters to them. For example, if you don't have really good product photos, if you manage to get a potential customer to visit your store, they won't click on a product listing and you won't generate sales," says Bold.

Another important ingredient for an Etsy® store's success is for the seller to always provide good customer service. "I always try to answer customer questions very quickly. It's also essential that you fulfill and ship orders in a timely manner. If you say you'll ship orders on the same day they're placed, this is something that you always need to follow through on. In a typical day, I spend at least two to three hours responding to customer emails and handling customer service-related issues and responsibilities.

"I typically respond to all new emails first thing every morning and then again in the late afternoon. In a typical week, I work at least 40 hours per week running my business. However, these days, I am only able to spend two to three hours per day, three days a week, actually creating new artwork. The rest of the time is spent doing other business-related tasks, like creating or updating product listings, taking product shots, and filling orders," she adds.

The next step in the growth and expansion of Bold's two Etsy® stores is for her to hire one or two part-time employees to handle the time-consuming business tasks so she can spend more time creating new artwork and developing new products. "For some reason, I am a little bit afraid to hire my first employees, but this is something I need to do to grow the business. For me, the biggest day-to-day challenge in operating two Etsy® stores is dealing with shipping issues and having to deal with shipping services that are out of my control. It's important to use a shipping service that allows you to track and insure all your shipments," explains Bold.

To help promote her business, Bold uses social media and maintains Facebook, Instagram, Pinterest, and Twitter accounts. She also maintains a blog that she uses to communicate with her customers, although she admits that she could put more time and effort into her online marketing efforts to achieve better results from them.

"I have had the most success promoting my artwork and products using Pinterest. This service seems to generate the most traffic to my Etsy® stores," she says. "In the past, I have toyed with paid online advertising, but this is not something I do consistently. For my business, I have found that focusing more time and effort on SEO has been much more lucrative than social media marketing, although this is different for every seller."

In terms of selling artwork on Etsy®, like so many sellers, Bold has discovered a lot of online competition. "I have found people who copy my artwork exactly and then sell it as their own. Over time, I have learned to ignore the competition and try to focus more on creating the best possible products I can. As a business operator, however, you should pay attention to the prices your competition is charging for similar items to what you're selling so that you can keep yourself competitive. If you do discover someone blatantly ripping off your work, Etsy® offers resources to help you protect your copyrights, trademarks, and intellectual property without having to initially hire a lawyer and incur high legal fees.

"Etsy® also offers tools to help sellers understand and analyze the traffic to their store. The SEO tools, for example, allow you to determine which keywords are driving traffic to your store and which are not. One drawback to Etsy® that I have found is that the service does not offer a bulk editing tool to quickly update or create multiple product listings simultaneously. If you have several hundred items in your store, this can be frustrating," adds Bold, who also needed to learn about bookkeeping and expense tracking to properly manage her business.

"I had no clue what I was doing when it came to maintaining accurate paperwork and handling the financial and tax-related tasks of my business. I learned by trial and error in the beginning. For new business operators, I definitely recommend acquiring these business skills as early on as possible. People need to realize that operating an Etsy® store to sell artwork online is a legitimate business, and it needs to be treated like one," she adds. "When I first started, I didn't understand that I needed to set money aside from my earnings for taxes. I recommend that when starting a business, you speak with an accountant who can help you handle the tax aspect of your business correctly. Otherwise, you could wind up with a very unpleasant surprise in the form of a high tax bill."

Another lesson Bold learned early on was how to charge appropriate shipping fees for her items. "You need to understand how much it will cost to ship your item and include package tracking and insurance. You also then need to have the appropriate shipping materials on hand when filling your orders. If you don't plan your shipping strategy correctly, the shipping charges can easily wind up costing double what you first thought, and you will wind up losing money. Make sure you use the right size shipping boxes, weigh everything correctly, and calculate your shipping charges in advance so you can charge the appropriate amount to your customers," she explains.

For new Etsy® sellers, Bold states, "Learn as much as you can before you get started, and then just go for it. Everything does not have to be perfect when you first launch your Etsy® store. You can always update and fine-tune things as you move forward. Don't overthink things to the point where you never create and open your shop. Overall, you'll probably find that the customers you get on Etsy® are awesome people who will support you as an artist and provide valuable feedback to you."

Additional Thoughts

How you interact with your customers (and potential customers) will ultimately play a huge role in your long-term success as a business operator. Happy customers might publish a positive review, refer others to your business, or become repeat customers themselves. Any (or all) of these three outcomes should be what you strive for with every person (customer or potential customer) you interact with. Offering top-notch customer service will help you grow your business over time. For more advice on growing your business, continue to the next chapter.

Growing Your Etsy® Business

A fter you initially create your Etsy® shop and open

for business, one of the following situations will

likely become obvious to you as a seller:

► Your business is growing and has become profit-

able. You're now ready to expand it. However, you're

not sure how to proceed or whether you're willing

to risk quitting your real-world, full-time job run your Etsy® shop on a full-time basis.

▶ To handle the demands of your growing and successful Etsy® business, you need to hire one or more part- or full-time employees or dedicate yourself to running your Etsy® shop and potentially spending considerably more than 40 hours per week to do so.

▶ You're having fun operating your Etsy® business enjoy the extra revenue it generates but want to keep the operation small and manageable. You may want to keep it as a part-time business venture or as a hobby that allows you to earn some extra money.

▶ You have built up a steady flow of paying customers and have maintained a positive relationship with these people, but now you need to expand your selection of products to generate repeat business or grow your customer base.

▶ To expand your target audience, you need to expand your product offerings yet maintain the focus of your shop and overall brand.

warning

Do not quit your income-producing, full-time or part-time job in the "real" world until your Etsy® shop has proven that it can consistently generate enough profit to fully support you financially. Having one or two profitable months in a row is a good indication of potential long-term success, but you want to see how things progress over at least six months to make sure the business allows you to generate a steady and predictable income.

▶ Based on the time, resources, and money you've already invested into the business and the feedback you have received, you believe you should be more successful. Thus, you want to generate a steadier flow of traffic to the shop and increase sales from the visitors to your shop by increasing your conversion rate.

▶ Based on how things have progressed, you've discovered that running an online business, even on a part-time basis, simply isn't for you.

Depending on which scenario best fits your situation, you'll want to think carefully about the steps you take next.

Once you believe you have the basics of running your Etsy® business mastered, or you're at least comfortable handling the day-to-day responsibilities required of you, this is when you should consider growing or expanding your business. It's typically best to take a slow and steady approach that involves minimal financial risk.

Based on the amount of profit you're consistently earning, you have a handful of options related to how you can expand or grow your operation. These include:

▶ Expanding your product line and introducing new products or new product variations (such as colors, sizes, or styles) that will allow you to gain more customers

▶ Increasing your marketing and advertising efforts so you can attract more customers and generate more sales for your existing products

▶ Brainstorming new ideas for products that are unrelated to your current offerings and opening a second or even a third Etsy® shop that you'll operate simultaneously with your original one. The new shop(s) would potentially sell a new and totally different selection of products to different target audiences.

▶ Hiring one or more part-time employees if you're maxed out on your personal resources and don't have the time to create new products, manage your shop, and fulfil orders on your own

▶ Quitting your "real-world" job to dedicate all your time and effort to the operation of your Etsy® shop

Always Keep Your Shop's Content Fresh

To help maintain a steady flow of visitors to your shop and increase your chances of earning repeat business from existing customers, you should refresh your shop every few months. This might mean updating all your text content and updating your product photography, tweaking the color scheme and overall visual appearance of the shop, and/or revising your product offerings. At the very least, it could mean using the Shop Updates feature of the Sell on Etsy® mobile app to add more product photography and product lifestyle shots to your shop on a regular basis.

Every three to four months (basically every season), carefully evaluate your sales from the previous quarter or season and determine which were your bestselling products and which items were the least popular. Seriously consider removing the least popular items from your shop altogether and putting more focus on items that are consistently popular.

At the same time, consider offering limited edition items or items that will only be available for a limited time. A "limited edition" item means you promote that only a predetermined number of that item will be made available, say 50 or 100. An item available for a limited time means that after a predetermined date, it will be removed from your shop and not offered again anytime in the near future.

tip

You always have the option to reintroduce a discontinued item, or an updated version of the discontinued item, at a later date.

tip

Your goals as a seller should be to update your shop multiple times throughout the year to keep its appearance and product selection fresh for your audience, while also maintaining your consistent brand.

Either one of these approaches adds a sense of urgency in the customer's mind plus allows you to introduce new products in a way that's more apt to get attention. You should also consider introducing seasonal items or items that are only available around specific holidays, such as Mother's Day, Father's Day, Valentine's Day, or Christmas.

In conjunction with popular holidays that your target audience will be shopping for, consider updating the overall appearance of your shop, including themed graphics, photos, and text that focuses on the upcoming holiday.

Holidays are also a great time to launch special sales or promotions. For example, during the Christmas holiday season, you could offer 10 to 25 percent off or free shipping. Perhaps a buy two and get a third free offer would appeal to your audience. You could also bundle groups of related products together and offer the bundle for a limited time at a discounted price in conjunction with a specific holiday.

Hosting sales or promotions is a quick, easy, and proven strategy for quickly boosting business, provided you're offering a good deal that your customers will appreciate. Be creative when planning sales or promotions, but don't make them too confusing.

As time passes and consumer trends and interests change, it's important that your shop keep up with this evolution. However, when it comes to updating your product offerings, don't make drastic changes to your entire product line at once. Instead, slowly introduce a few new items while phasing out older, less popular items. By studying your target audience and paying attention to feedback you receive from customers, deciding what subtle product changes to make should become rather straightforward as time goes on.

The key to growing your business over the long term is to understand that your shop should be continuously evolving and should not remain stagnant for more than a month. Ideally, you should continuously update or tweak content, such as product listings and product photos, even if the actual products you're selling remain constant for an entire season or longer.

tip

Each time you refresh your shop, be sure to update your keywords, titles, and text content to help with SEO and potentially reach a larger group of people that still fits into your target audience.

Moving forward, don't ever make changes to your shop haphazardly. Develop an organized approach or plan for your shop and product line updates, and then stick to it. Before making any change, determine why you're making it, what impact you want it to have, what your goals are, and what impact the changes will have on your shop's visitors. Remember to consider your target audience and anticipate how they'll react to the changes.

Seven Ways to Expand Your Business

The easiest way to handle growth to your business is when it happens slowly and organically. Over time, you reach a broader audience with your advertising and marketing, drive more traffic to your shop, and then figure out ways to improve your conversion rate (transforming visitors into paying customers).

Some of the proven ways you can grow your business when you're ready include:

1. Increase the number of items you offer by adding more product listings to your shop. But be sure to keep your product offerings somewhat related. For example, if you already sell bracelets, necklaces, and earrings, consider adding a line of rings. Don't offer random, unrelated products that won't appeal to your core audience. For example, don't add clothing or housewares to your shop that showcases and sells your jewelry product line. What you can do, however, is introduce a higher-end or premium selection of related products that are sold at a higher price point. For example, if you already sell silver jewelry, consider offering the same designs in 24k gold.

2. Improve the quality of your product photography. In addition to making the photos look better, consider adjusting your use of traditional product shots and lifestyle shots to better showcase each of your items.

3. Consider expanding your target audience. You already know who your core target audience is and should be marketing and advertising to that audience. While you continue to do this, pinpoint a secondary target audience and begin separate marketing and advertising efforts to reach this new or broader group of people.

4. If you haven't already done so, open your shop to international customers and be willing to ship internationally (assuming what you're selling will have international appeal).

5. Increase the amount of money you're investing in online paid advertising, and consider trying additional advertising opportunities. At the same time, boost your social media presence.

6. Consider sales opportunities beyond Etsy®. Once you have developed a proven and strong market, consider participating in craft fairs, for example, or expanding to sell your products through mainstream retail stores, boutiques, specialty shops, consignment shops, and/or other online services. Keep in mind, however, that retailers will need to buy products from you at wholesale prices (which are typically half your retail price), so make sure doing this will allow your business to remain profitable.

7. As the need arises for you to create your product(s) in larger quantities, develop faster or more efficient ways to save time in the creation or manufacturing process. This might mean making an investment in better tools, for example. At the same time, try to lower your cost for acquiring your raw materials/supplies. For example, buy your materials/supplies from a wholesaler or directly from the manufacturer in larger quantities to receive a bigger discount.

Consider Expansion to Other Services

As you read in Chapter 1, there are other online services (such as Amazon Handmade) that cater to artisans and crafters. Each of them has their own loyal following of shoppers (and potential customers for you). As your success grows, you might consider expanding your online presence by starting a similar storefront on one or more of these competing services to potentially reach a broader audience.

However, your best bet is to start with just one service (Etsy® or Amazon Handmade, for example). Look to get your business running and successful before you branch out onto other platforms. You will find that competing services offer different fee structures for sellers as well as a different selection of tools that allow you to customize your storefront. For example, running a storefront on multiple platforms will make your inventory control and bookkeeping more challenging. This book focuses on Etsy® because it's currently the most popular and successful platform of its kind for artisans and crafters.

Another option is to create your own, standalone ecommerce website, which gives you the ability to fully customize everything having to do with your online store. Whether you choose to expand your online presence by opening storefronts on other services or starting your own standalone website, make sure your Etsy® storefront is operating efficiently and that you've maximized what's possible on this platform. Otherwise, you will likely find that running multiple storefronts on different services becomes time-consuming and confusing.

Meet Andrew Church, Proprietor of Bison Hill Stonecrafts

Andrew Church is a reliability engineer with GE Transportation with a master's degree in mechanical engineering from Pennsylvania State University. While he is very happy with how his full-time career is going, back in 2014, he also chose to create an Etsy® store, called Bison Hill Stonecrafts (www.Etsy.com/shop/BisonHillStonecrafts), through which he sells a variety of handcrafted products made from slate and marble. Figure 8–1 shows the main page of the Bison Hill Stonecrafts shop.

The idea for his business came about while he was looking for a way to create a custom design within a slate roof. He purchased a diamond band saw for several hundred dollars and started playing with it. This is when he discovered how intricately he could cut slate and how versatile the slate material is.

Initially for fun, he started making ornaments, cutting boards, cheese boards, coasters, house numbers, and other items made from hand-cut slate. Several of his friends suggested he start selling his creations, which gave him the idea to create an Etsy® shop.

"I had never been on Etsy® before but stumbled on it while doing my research. I thought it would be the perfect place to sell my crafts without all of the pressure of having

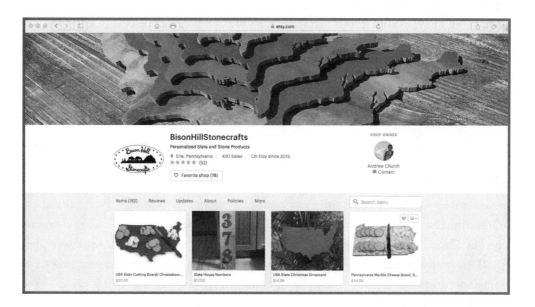

FIGURE 8–1: **Bison Hill Stonecrafts**
This Etsy® shop showcases a selection of handcrafted items made from slate and other materials.

to design an ecommerce website from scratch. I figured this would be a great way to dip my toe in the water and experience entrepreneurship for the first time," recalls Church, who never liked art classes that were offered at his elementary, middle, or high school when he was younger.

"In college, I took a pottery class. That's when I started to develop my artistic side. I really enjoyed doing pottery work, and after that, I sstarted to do some painting. The pottery class caused me to start exploring hobbies that interested me. Since then, I have become more crafty. Now I really enjoy working with slate," he says. "In my store, many of my products are slate that has been cut into the shape of a state and then laser-engraved with a personalized message or the customer's name."

In the early days of his Etsy® store, which he started with an initial investment of about $500 in equipment and supplies, Church went through what he refers to as an explosive creative phase. He experimented with all sorts of different product ideas, all made from slate.

"Many of my products can be used for food preparation or dining, whether it's a cheese plate, cutting board, serving platter, or coaster set, but I have also created items like earrings and wind chimes from slate," he says.

At the time Church stumbled on Etsy® and created his Etsy® store, he didn't know about any other platforms that would allow him to easily set up a shop and sell his creations. "I knew about eBay, of course, but that didn't feel like it would be the best place to sell my products. I thought of eBay as the place you go to sell off your old crap, and I thought of Amazon as being very commercialized. Etsy® seemed like the perfect fit for me to build my brand," adds Church. "Much more recently, I have also been tinkering with creating my own website, using the Shopify platform, and selling on Amazon Handmade as well. We'll see how that goes, but I have no plans to abandon Etsy®."

According to Church, the target customer for Bison Hill Stonecrafts is middle-aged women. "These people make up about 75 percent of my sales. These are the people who seem to care the most about entertaining, decorating, and creative gift-giving. A lot of my products are bought for the customer's own home, or they're given as a gift by my customers to someone else. It's mainly the women who decorate the living room and dining room, or who buy Christmas tree ornaments to decorate their family tree during the holidays.

"Most of my customers are already frequent shoppers on Etsy®. I do have some hunting-themed products that are targeted to men, but those have not sold very well because I have not yet figured out how to drive men to my Etsy® store. I tried Google AdWords advertising, for example, in order to target men, but the response was not what I had hoped," he adds. "As a result, I have focused on the products that I know women prefer to buy."

Initially, when Church was setting up his Etsy® store, he simply followed the steps outlined by the Etsy® website. He didn't do anything special to refine his tags or focus on search engine optimization, for example. He just filled in the fields with the information that was requested.

"For me, it was an easy, relatively quick, learn-as-you-go experience. It took me a few hours to get the store set up and create my first few product listings. It took much longer, however, to actually get my first sale. During the first week the store was online, I received no store views. After that, store views would trickle in. It actually took almost three months for me to receive my first sale," he recalls. "I did nothing initially to market or promote my Etsy® store. I just waited for traffic to filter in naturally. Looking back, I would have done some online ads and marketing to increase traffic to the store early on."

During the time he was waiting for his first sale, Church invested time to tweak the content of his shop, improving the tags, product titles, and product descriptions he was featuring and reshooting many of his initial product photographs.

"My first product photos were shot on my smartphone with no special background or lighting. I just took random pictures of the products and published them online. Once I started to improve the quality of my photos, that featured a white background and good lighting, I think this is when I noticed traffic to my store really increase," says Church.

When Church launched his Etsy® store, he dreamed of becoming a millionaire from his online business. He recalls, "I had those fantasies. I hoped I could become one of those few people who launch an Etsy® store and wind up quitting their job after a few months so they can sell their crafts full time and earn a good living from their Etsy® store. It's just not like that in real life, however. It takes a lot of time, effort, and dedication to grow a successful Etsy® store. Nothing happens overnight or without the seller putting in the required effort. It's important to develop realistic expectations right from the start. Overall, I think Etsy® is really great, and once I developed realistic expectations, the Etsy® platform lived up to them."

In addition to having really good product photography, Church believes the tags a seller uses need to be carefully selected and relevant. "A seller needs to think like a buyer and choose tags that accurately describe their products. A seller needs to come up with words that describe their product in a way that will target their intended audience. Also, in each of your product descriptions, you need to include basic and relevant information about the product. For me, this includes what the product is made of, its dimensions, why it's needed, and how to care for it. Provide information that a customer will want to know and make it easy for your potential customers who want to buy your products," says Church.

In terms of branding, Church designed his own company logo. "I think having a logo that looks good is important, but you don't need to spend a fortune to have a professional graphic artist custom design your logo. I think the product photos are far more important than the logo. The Etsy® store for Bison Hill Stonecrafts offers a very rustic appearance and design. So in my product shots, for example, I try to incorporate earth tones and reclaimed barn wood, which compliments the appearance of the handcrafted slate items," he adds.

Based on his experience selling on Etsy®, Church believes that striving to earn five-star reviews is critically important. "In addition to giving you credibility as a seller, having consistent five-star reviews gives a prospective customer added assurance. I believe five-star reviews also help boost your ranking when potential customers do searches on Etsy®," explains Church. "Many people will buy your products and love them but won't follow through and write a review. I think there's a fine line between asking for a review and pestering your customers for a review. The approach I take is to use email in order to ask for feedback about the product, and then, I gently remind customers to submit their review."

Church lives on a 100-plus-acre farm near Erie, Pennsylvania, and has always been fascinated by bison. His dream is to someday soon set up a pasture and have bison on his farm in addition to cows. "I named a hill in the back of my house Bison Hill, which is where the name of the business came from. These days, I spend a lot of my time creating and updating my product listings and keeping my product photos current and fresh. To help with these mundane efforts, I hired a high school student to help me part time. This allowed me to focus more time on creating products and doing marketing for my store, as opposed to store maintenance.

"I maintain my full-time job and operate Bison Hill Stonecrafts on the side. This eats into my free time, but the time investment is well worth it," says Church, who now spends 15 to 20 hours per week handling all aspects of his business. "This time includes doing online marketing and advertising on social media."

In addition to paid advertising on Etsy®, Church does paid Facebook advertising. "Paid ads have always been worth it for me, but it's not something I do consistently. Some months it pays off more than others. I spend about $50 per month in paid online advertising. I maintain a company Facebook page as well as a presence on Instagram," he says. "As an engineer, I never really focused on writing as a skill. This is something I've needed to develop since starting my business. Using descriptive words and flowery writing is essential when creating content for an Etsy® store."

Before someone launches their own Etsy® store, Church recommends that first-time sellers do research, figure out what's already out there, and then really focus on creative ways to do things better and differently.

"You have to be able to set yourself apart as a seller or you're going to get lost. You need to come up with a unique twist to your approach or come up with a clever way to market what you're selling to your target audience. Don't try to sell something to a mass market audience. You really need to focus on a niche audience that you can clearly define. Once you figure out what works for your target audience, you can always expand to other niche audiences. However, you need to laser-focus your efforts toward a specific audience," says Church.

Based on his experience running his own online business, Church warns people following in his footsteps that there's a lot of misinformation online. "When doing your research and learning how to do various things, like search engine optimization, you need to find and rely on credible sources. I have read some extremely stupid things online about SEO that could be more harmful than helpful. The *Etsy® Seller Handbook* [www.Etsy.com/seller-handbook], however, is loaded with useful information for first-time sellers that pertains directly to the Etsy® platform," says Church.

As he spends more and more time working on Bison Hill Stonecrafts, he becomes less and less reliant on the income from his full-time job. "For me, it's a great feeling to know that if I ever get laid off from my main job, I already have an established business I can fall back on," he concludes.

Final Thoughts

Whatever it is you decide to sell on Etsy® (assuming it fits within Etsy®'s ever-expanding list of acceptable product types), remember that the internet, the Etsy® platform, the technology people use to access Etsy® as buyers (whether it's their computer, smartphone, or tablet), as well as consumer online shopping trends and habits, are always evolving and changing. As an Etsy® seller, it's important you stay current with this evolution as well as the changing wants and needs of your customers.

As trends change, your selling approach and the content of your shop should evolve as well. For example, these days, more and more buyers are using the Etsy® mobile app to find and shop for items. The mobile app runs on smartphones and tablets that have smaller screens than notebook or desktop computers. Thus, as a seller, you want to format your text, and adjust your photos, so it's all visually appealing and easy to see regardless of the screen size it's being viewed on.

Meanwhile, if someone is using their smartphone to shop, chances are it's while they're on the go, standing in line for their coffee, or during their commute to work, for example. Their time and attention span is more limited than ever. As a seller, this means you have less time to pique someone's interest and convert them from being just a visitor to your shop into a paying customer.

In addition to knowing and truly understanding the product(s) you're selling and being able to tell a compelling story, it's more important than ever to be able to communicate a lot of relevant information concisely and quickly in a way that fits nicely with your target customer's shopping habits.

If your plan is to create an Etsy® shop, populate it with some product listings and then just sit back and wait for the orders to come in, you're going to be very disappointed with the results. Right from the start, understand that everything related to your Etsy® business needs to be considered an ever-evolving work in progress, which will need to be updated regularly.

You also will need to market, promote, and advertise your shop on an ongoing basis, using a variety of different (and simultaneous) approaches to drive a continuous flow of traffic to your shop.

All this is in addition to creating and maintaining your shop's inventory, while also trying to brainstorm ideas for new, unusual, or unique products/items to introduce in your shop. This may all sound a bit daunting at first, but if you consider the thousands of successful Etsy® sellers who have come before you, you'll probably determine that you, too, can handle the challenges and responsibilities of operating an Etsy® shop.

Etsy® Business Resources

The following list includes website addresses for quickly accessing additional information about specific topics covered in this book and that are of direct interest to Etsy® sellers. These resources are listed in alphabetical order. Details about each website, online service, or resource are covered in this book's various chapters.

▶ 99Designs: www.99designs.com/projects

▶ Adobe Stock: https://stock.adobe.com

▶ Adorama: www.adorama.com

▶ Amazon Handmade

▶ B&H Photo/Video: www.bhphotovideo.com

- ▶ Best of the Web Blog Search: https://blogs.botw.org

- ▶ Bing Ads: https://advertise.bingads.microsoft.com

- ▶ Blog Catalog: www.blogcatalog.com

- ▶ Blog Search Engine: www.blogsearchengine.com

- ▶ Bloggapedia: www.bloggapedia.com

- ▶ Blogger.com: www.blogger.com

- ▶ BlogListing: www.bloglisting.net

- ▶ Bonanza: www.bonanza.com/sell_products_online

- ▶ Boomerang: www.boomerang.com

- ▶ Campaigner: www.campaigner.com

- ▶ Constant Contact: www.constantcontact.com/email-marketing

- ▶ DaWanda: www.dawanda.com

- ▶ DesignCrowd: www.designcrowd.com

- ▶ EatonWeb: The Blog Directory: http://portal.eatonweb.com

- ▶ EcoDash Inventory Tracking Software: www.ecomdash.com/inventory-management-software/

- ▶ eReleases: www.ereleases.com

- ▶ Etsy® Advertising: www.Etsy.com/help/article/49716927767

- ▶ Etsy® Advertising Information: www.Etsy.com/advertising

- ▶ Etsy® Manufacturing Resources: www.Etsy.com/manufacturing

- ▶ Etsy® Mobile App Information: www.Etsy.com/apps

- ▶ Etsy® Product Photography Information: www.Etsy.com/seller-handbook/category/photography

- ▶ Etsy® Promoted Listings Information: www.Etsy.com/help/article/49190700688

- ▶ Etsy® Reader Information: www.Etsy.com/reader

- ▶ *Etsy® Seller Handbook*: www.Etsy.com/seller-handbook

▶ Etsy® Shipping Costs Information: www.Etsy.com/help/article/6131

▶ Etsy® Shipping Profile Information: www.Etsy.com/help/article/190

▶ Etsy® Shop Discount Codes Information: www.Etsy.com/help/article/349

▶ Etsy® Shop Sections Information: www.Etsy.com/help/article/165

▶ Etsy® Shop Updates Information: www.Etsy.com/seller-handbook/article/5-tips-for-sharing-your-story-with-shop/31380092335

▶ Etsy®'s Seller Forums: www.Etsy.com/forums

▶ Etsy®'s Online Labs (instructional videos): www.Etsy.com/community/online-labs

▶ Etsy®'s Help Center: www.Etsy.com/help

▶ Facebook: www.facebook.com

▶ Facebook Advertising: www.facebook.com/business

▶ Fishbowl Small Business Inventory: www.fishbowlinventory.com/articles/inventory-management/small-business-inventory-software

▶ Fiverr: www.fiverr.com

▶ Freelancer.com: www.freelancer.com/?t=b&utm_expid=294858-533.sSCN-RzLRZK-gGrc0_aFaw.1#

▶ GetResponse: www.getresponse.com

▶ Google AdWords Advertising: www.google.com/AdWords

▶ GovSimplified: www.taxid-gov.us

▶ Handmadeology: www.handmadeology.com

▶ iCraft Gifts: www.icraftgifts.com/sell.php

▶ Instagram: www.instagram.com

▶ Instagram Advertising: https://business.instagram.com/advertising

▶ Internal Revenue Service: www.irs.gov/uac/business-or-hobby-answer-has-implications-for-deductions

▶ Internal Revenue Service (SS-4 Form Download): www.irs.gov/pub/irs-pdf/fss4.pdf

▶ iStockPhoto: www.istockphoto.com

- ▶ JumpStock Inventory Management: www.jumptech.com/products/jumpstock

- ▶ LegalZoom: www.legalzoom.com

- ▶ LegalZoom DBA Filing Information: www.legalzoom.com/business/business-formation/dba-overview.html

- ▶ LinkedIn: www.linkedin.com

- ▶ LivePlan: www.LivePlan.com

- ▶ MailChimp: www.mailchimp.com

- ▶ Model Mayhem: www.modelmayhem.com

- ▶ O'Dwyer's PR Firm Directory: www.odwyerpr.com/pr_firms_database/index.htm

- ▶ OnToplist: www.ontoplist.com

- ▶ Pinterest: www.pinterest.com

- ▶ PR Newswire: www.prnewswire.com

- ▶ PRChannel: www.prchannel.com

- ▶ PRWeb: www.prweb.com

- ▶ Public Relations Society of America: www.prsa.org

- ▶ QuickBook Point of Sale Software: www.intuitpayments.com/seg/brand/all/qb-pointofsale

- ▶ Shutterstock: www.shutterstock.com

- ▶ SimpleFilings: www.simplefilings.com/state-dba/home.php

- ▶ SimplyHired: www.simplyhired.com

- ▶ Social Media Wire: http://socialmediawire.net

- ▶ Tumblr: www.tumblr.com

- ▶ Twitter: www.twitter.com

- ▶ Twitter Advertising: https://ads.twitter.com

- ▶ Upwork: www.upwork.com

- ▶ U.S. Small Business Administration Business Plan Creation Tools: www.sba.gov/starting-business/write-your-business-plan

▶ WordPress: https://wordpress.org

▶ Yahoo! Advertising: https://advertising.yahoo.com

▶ YouTube: www.youtube.com

▶ YouTube Creator Hub: www.youtube.com/yt/creators

▶ YouTube Help: www.youtube.com/user/youtubehelp

▶ Zibbet: www.zibbet.com/sell

Glossary

Amazon Handmade: An online service operated by Amazon that allows crafters, artists, artisans, and creative people to showcase and sell their items by creating an online store. Amazon Handmade is one of several companies competing with Etsy® that offer a marketplace and turnkey selling solution for creative entrepreneurs.

ApplePay: A third-party digital payment service operated by Apple that allows buyers to make secure debit or credit card purchases from their computer, iPhone, or iPad while shopping on Etsy®.

Blog: A digital diary that allows the blogger (the author of the blog) to share posts that they compose in a public online forum. Etsy® sellers often use a blog to communicate informally with their customers and people interested in their products. A blog can take on the form of a digital newsletter, for example. Each blog entry is dated and can include text, photos, video clips, links to webpages, and other types of content. Blog entries are displayed for the viewer in chronological order. Creating and managing a blog is typically free and easy to manage as no website programming is required. This can be done using a service such as Blogger, Wordpress, Tumblr, or a Facebook for Business page, for example.

Buyer: A person who shops on Etsy® who will visit an Etsy® shop to browse or make a purchase.

Category: Based on what's being sold in an Etsy® shop, sellers are encouraged to choose from a predefined list of categories into which their shop fits best. Choosing the most appropriate categories makes it easier for buyers to find your shop.

Conversion Rate: The percentage of the traffic to an Etsy® shop that actually becomes paying customers. Only a small percentage of the people who visit an Etsy® shop will become a paying customer. It's up to the seller to customize their shop's content to increase the conversion rate and constantly strive to make it as high as possible.

Domain Registrar: An independent service, such as GoDaddy, that allows people to register a custom domain name to be used by an Etsy® shop, website, blog, or online store, for example. A custom URL must be unique but can end with a wide range of extensions, such as .com, .info, .photo, or .store. A separate annual fee, typically under $20, applies when registering each domain name.

Etsy® Community: The large and ever-growing group of buyers and sellers that use Etsy® and maintain free Etsy® accounts. Anyone can set up a free account, join the Etsy® community, and then make purchases from sellers or set up their own Etsy® shop to showcase and sell their items.

Etsy® Mobile App: Etsy®'s official smartphone and tablet app used to shop on Etsy® and manage an account.

Etsy® Profile: Every member of the Etsy® community is encouraged to create a personal profile that displays their photo. It also includes some personal information. Sellers are encouraged to expand their profile to tell their story and share more information about themselves as an artist, artisan, or crafter, as well as their work.

Etsy® Rating: When a buyer makes a purchase, they are able to rate a seller and the product(s) they've acquired, using between one and five stars (with five stars being the highest possible rating). Ratings are displayed in every Etsy® shop and are used by buyers to help them choose the best and most reputable shops and sellers to make purchases from.

Etsy® Reader: The credit card reader attachment for a smartphone or tablet that's offered by Etsy® and that allows sellers to accept and process in-person debit/credit card payments.

Etsy® Reviews: When a buyer makes a purchase, they are able to write a review of the Etsy® shop and the product(s) they've purchased. This allows the buyer to share their own thoughts and opinions. Reviews get published in the seller's shop and can be viewed by all future traffic and customers visiting that shop. Reviews are used by buyers to help them choose what to purchase and which sellers to make purchases from.

Etsy® Seller Handbook: The online resource compiled by Etsy® that offers comprehensive information for sellers about how to create, manage, promote, and expand their Etsy® shop. This is a free tool that continuously gets updated with new articles and information. Visit www.Etsy.com/seller-handbook.

Etsy® Shop: A virtual and customizable storefront on the Etsy® platform from which a seller can showcase and sell their items. A shop can display a logo, a selection of customizable content elements, and as many individual product listings as the seller desires. Etsy® shops are also referred to as Etsy® stores.

Etsy® Store: A virtual and customizable storefront on the Etsy® platform from which a seller can showcase and sell their items. A shop can display a logo, a selection of customizable content elements, and as many individual product listings as the seller desires. Etsy® stores are also referred to as Etsy® shops.

Facebook Advertising: Facebook offers the opportunity to advertise to a highly targeted audience on the Facebook service using a pay-per-click model. Etsy® sellers can use Facebook advertising as a fee-based way to quickly drive traffic to their Etsy® shop or to promote a specific product listing.

Google AdWords: An online paid advertising tool that allows sellers to feature their shop or product(s) when shoppers perform an internet search using Google or when they visit participating Google partner websites that display AdWords ads. Using Google AdWords allows sellers to reach a highly targeted audience and quickly drive traffic to their Etsy® shop. This is a very affordable and flexible paid advertising tool.

Lifestyle Photo: A type of product photo that showcases an item being used in the real world. For example, a lifestyle photo for jewelry might feature a person wearing the jewelry, while a typical product photo would showcase just the jewelry (close up) seen against a solid color (or simple) background.

Listing Fee: A flat fee of $0.20 is charged by Etsy® to the seller for each individual product listing that's added to a shop. This fee is charged when the product listing is created. Etsy®'s other fees to sellers are charged only after each sale is made.

Pay-Per-Click: This refers to how some online advertising services charge advertisers. Instead of prepaying for a specific number of views or impressions for an ad, pay-per-click allows advertisers to pay a predetermined fee each time someone sees their ad and clicks on the included link to visit an Etsy® shop or a specific product listing. Pay-per-click is used by Etsy®, Facebook, Instagram, Twitter, and Google AdWords, for example, all of which offer viable and highly targetable advertising opportunities for Etsy® sellers.

PayPal: A third-party digital payment service that handles credit and debit card transactions securely on behalf of the seller. A per-transaction fee applies.

Product Listing: Information about a single product that a seller is offering in their Etsy® shop. Each product listing can be accompanied by up to five product photos as well as textual information describing the product, a headline (title), and tags (keywords) that are used to describe the item being sold. A product listing can also include seller-specified variations, which allow buyers to select customizations for a product, such as a color or size, for example.

Product Photo: A typical product photo showcases a product being sold within an Etsy® shop. Up to five different photos can be used to show the product in greater detail or from various angles, for example. The goal of the product photos is to display as much detail as possible. Presenting top-quality, well-lit, and professional-looking images is extremely important.

Product Variation: Options set up by the seller that allow a buyer to select from predetermined options related to the item they're buying. Multiple variations can be set up for each product, allowing the buyer to choose a size, color, or some other customizable or selectable option.

Promoted Listing: A seller has the opportunity to pay Etsy® for a Promoted Listing, which means their product listing(s) will be more prominently displayed in a buyer's search results when browsing Etsy®. This is a way for sellers to get more attention and drive more traffic to their shop.

Return/Refund Policy: The policies established by the seller giving the customer (buyer) the option to return or exchange their purchases. Some sellers have an "all sales are final" policy and do not accept returns or exchanges, while others give customers up to 30 or 60 days to request a refund or exchange a product they've purchased from an Etsy® shop.

Section: A way of sorting and organizing groups of related product listings within an Etsy® shop. Sellers can create as many custom sections as they deem necessary to make it easier for buyers to quickly find the items they're looking for. For example, a seller who offers jewelry might feature separate shop sections labeled "Bracelets," "Necklaces," "Rings," and "Earrings."

Sell on Etsy® Mobile App: The official Etsy® app used by sellers to manage their shop remotely from a smartphone or tablet.

Seller: The person who uses the Etsy® platform to create, host, and manage an Etsy® shop to showcase and sell their items.

Shipping Policies: The options offered by Etsy® sellers that allow buyers (customers) to select a shipping preference and method for their purchase. The seller can choose how they're willing to ship items domestically and/or internationally and what shipping options will be offered (such as ground shipping, second-day shipping, or overnight shipping). The seller also decides if free shipping will be included with orders or if customers will be charged an extra shipping and handling fee when placing their order.

Shop Name: The name a seller gives to their Etsy® shop, which must be unique and contain between four and 20 characters but not include any spaces. A combination of upper- and lowercase letters can be used within a shop name. The shop name is prominently displayed in each shop in conjunction with the optional company logo that the seller provides and uploads.

Shop URL: The unique website address assigned to an Etsy® shop once it's been created and established on the Etsy® platform. Every shop must have a unique shop name and is provided with a unique website URL.

Social Media: Online services like Facebook, Instagram, Twitter, Pinterest, Tumblr, Snapchat, and YouTube that can be used by Etsy® sellers to informally communicate with prospective and paying customers to promote their shop and items.

Tag: A selection of keywords the seller links with a product listing that accurately describes their product or item. Tags are used as part of Etsy®'s search engine optimization tools to make it easier for buyers to find shops and product listings they're interested in based on the keyword searches they perform using the Etsy® platform's search tool.

Target Audience: The group of people who you define to be the perfect customers for whatever it is you're selling. A target audience can be defined by any number of factors, such as age, sex, religion, geographic location, race, income, education level, occupation, or the hobbies someone enjoys. As a seller, you want to define your niche audience as precisely and accurately as possible.

Tax Identification Number: In the process of setting up your Etsy® shop as a legal business entity with the U.S. government, a tax identification number is required for your business (if you're based in the United States). This will be used when filing your tax returns and entitles business operators to set up a bank account for their company plus more easily buy supplies and materials at wholesale prices from wholesalers, distributors, and manufacturers. Depending on how you set up your business, your Tax Identification Number may be the Etsy® shop owner's Social Security number.

Title: The headline given to each product listing created by a seller. Each headline should be descriptive, concise, accurate, and attention-getting.

Traffic: This refers to the number of people who visit an Etsy® shop within a day, week, or month, for example. Only a small percentage of this traffic will actually make a purchase and become a paying customer, however.

Transaction Fees: The fees that Etsy® charges the seller each time a buyer makes a purchase from their shop. These fees, in addition to the product listing fees, should be included in your cost of goods sold when calculating your retail prices for items being sold in your Etsy® store.

U.S. Copyright Office: The department within the U.S. government at which an individual or a business files a copyright registration. For more information, visit www.copyright.gov.

U.S. Patent and Trademark Office: The department of the U.S. government at which an individual or a business files a patent or trademark. For more information, visit www.uspto.gov.

Index